The Indian Wars

From Frontier to Reservation

Titles in the History's Great Defeats series include:

HISTORY'S
GREAT DEFEATS

The Indian Wars

From Frontier to Reservation

by Don Nardo

Lucent Books, San Diego, CA

No part of this book may be reproduced or used in any form or by any means, electrical, mechanical, or otherwise, including, but not limited to, photocopy, recording, or any information storage and retrieval system, without prior written permission from the publisher.

Library of Congress Cataloging-in-Publication Data

Nardo, Don, 1947–
    The Indian wars : from frontier to reservation / by Don Nardo.
        p. cm. — (History's great defeats)
    Includes bibliographical references and index.
    ISBN 1-56006-891-4 (hardback : acid-free paper)
    1. Indians of North America—Wars—Juvenile literature. [1. Indians of North America—Wars.] I. Title. II. Series.
    E81 .N38   2002
    970—dc21

2001001540

Table of Contents

Foreword

HISTORY IS FILLED with tales of dramatic encounters that sealed the fates of empires or civilizations, changing them or causing them to disappear forever. One of the best known events began in 334 B.C., when Alexander, king of Macedonia, led his small but formidable Greek army into Asia. In the short span of only ten years, he brought Persia, the largest empire the world had yet seen, to its knees, earning him the nickname forever after associated with his name—"the Great." The demise of Persia, which at its height stretched from the shores of the Mediterranean Sea in the west to the borders of India in the east, was one of history's most stunning defeats. It occurred primarily because of some fatal flaws in the Persian military system, disadvantages the Greeks had exploited before, though never as spectacularly as they did under Alexander.

First, though the Persians had managed to conquer many peoples and bring huge territories under their control, they had failed to create an individual fighting man who could compare with the Greek hoplite. A heavily armored infantry soldier, the hoplite fought in a highly effective and lethal battlefield formation—the phalanx. Possessed of better armor, weapons, and training than the Persians, Alexander's soldiers repeatedly crushed their Persian opponents. Second, the Persians for the most part lacked generals of the caliber of their Greek counterparts. And when Alexander invaded, Persia had the added and decisive disadvantage of facing one of the greatest generals of all time. When the Persians were defeated, their great empire was lost forever.

Other world powers and civilizations have fallen in a like manner. They have succumbed to some combination of inherent fatal flaws or

6

disadvantages, to political and/or military mistakes, and even to the personal failings of their leaders.

Another of history's great defeats was the sad demise of the North American Indian tribes at the hands of encroaching European civilization from the sixteenth to nineteenth centuries. In this case, all of the tribes suffered from the same crippling disadvantages. Among the worst, they lacked the great numbers, the unity, and the advanced industrial and military hardware possessed by the Europeans. Still another example, one closer to our own time, was the resounding defeat of Nazi Germany by the Allies in 1945, which brought World War II, the most disastrous conflict in history, to a close. Nazi Germany collapsed for many reasons. But one of the most telling was that its leader, Adolf Hitler, sorely underestimated the material resources and human resolve of the Allies, especially the United States. In the end, Germany was in a very real sense submerged by a massive and seemingly relentless tidal wave of Allied bombs, tanks, ships, and soldiers.

Seen in retrospect, a good many of the fatal flaws, drawbacks, and mistakes that caused these and other great defeats from the pages of history seem obvious. It is only natural to wonder why, in each case, the losers did not realize their limitations and/or errors sooner and attempt to avert disaster. But closer examination of the events, social and political trends, and leading personalities involved usually reveals that complex factors were at play. Arrogance, fear, ignorance, stubbornness, innocence, and other attitudes held by nations, peoples, and individuals often colored and shaped their reactions, goals, and strategies. And it is both fascinating and instructive to reconstruct how such attitudes, as well as the fatal flaws and mistakes themselves, contributed to the losers' ultimate demise.

Each volume in Lucent Books' *History's Great Defeats* series is designed to provide the reader with diverse learning tools for exploring the topic at hand. Each well-informed, clearly written text is supported and enlivened by substantial quotes by the actual people involved, as well as by later historians and other experts; and these primary and secondary sources are carefully documented. Each volume also supplies the reader with an extensive Works Consulted list, guiding him or her to further research on the topic. These and other research tools, including glossaries and time lines, afford the reader a thorough understanding of how and why one of history's most decisive defeats occurred and how these events shaped our world.

"Our Indian Life Is Gone Forever"

Introduction

IN 1785, WHILE SERVING as U.S. minister to France, Thomas Jefferson published his *Notes on the State of Virginia*, a detailed description of his native state. Among the many and diverse anecdotes and quotations he included in the work was a speech by a Native American leader named Tachnedorus, who was more commonly known among whites as John Logan. Logan, a chief of the Mingo tribe, had at first been a friend of the local whites. But when they murdered his wife and children, he turned on them; and he was among the Indians defeated by the English in Lord Dunmore's War in 1774. Soon afterward, as Jefferson reported, Logan defended his actions, saying:

> I appeal to any white man to say, if ever he entered Logan's cabin hungry, and he gave him not meat; if ever he came cold and naked, and he clothed him not. . . . Such was my love for the whites, that my countrymen pointed as they passed, and said, "Logan is a friend of the white men.". . . [But then] last spring, in cold blood, and unprovoked, [the whites] murdered all the relations of Logan, not sparing even my women and children. There runs not a drop of my blood in the veins of any living creature. This called on me for revenge. . . . For my country, I rejoice at the beams of peace. But do not harbor a thought that mine is the joy of fear. Logan never felt fear. He will not turn on his heel to save his life. Who is there to mourn for Logan? Not one.[1]

This moving speech, which became known as "Logan's Lament," might well serve as an epitaph for all the Native American tribes and individuals who fought the United States in the century

8

that followed. Many, like Logan, at first sought to befriend their new white neighbors. But they soon learned that the whites were not content with peaceful coexistence. In the wake of a long series of lies and broken treaties on the part of the whites, many tribes bravely resisted white encroachment onto Indian lands. And one by one, each met with the same fate—defeat and subjugation.

The cost of the defeat of Native Americans by the United States was enormous and devastating. Before white Europeans began colonizing North America, the area now encompassed by the continental United States was inhabited by at least 1 million Indians, organized into some six hundred separate, flourishing tribes. By the time the Indian Wars ended in the 1890s, dozens of tribes had been totally or nearly eradicated. The rest had been decimated and demoralized. The exact death toll inflicted by the United States from the time of the American Revolution to the 1890s is difficult to assess. But drawing on data from various sources, including the U.S. government itself, University of Minnesota scholar Russell Thornton estimates

Pictured at right is Tachnedorus, known to whites as John Logan. Depicted in the woodcut below, is the massacre of his family by whites.

45,000 American Indians killed in wars with Europeans and Americans between 1775 and 1890. To this might be added the . . . 8,500 American Indians killed in individual conflicts during the period, to arrive at a total of 53,500 killed, by the U.S. government's own admission. . . . American Indians were also killed by other Indians in intertribal wars resulting from European involvement in tribal relations. As these deaths are added, the mortality figures become considerably more substantial: 150,000? 250,000? 500,000? We do not know.[2]

Whatever the actual number of Native Americans killed, it is unarguable that the impact of the white conquest on their culture was disastrous. Whole peoples were uprooted and forced to leave their ancestral homelands forever. "Their lands, gone," scholars John Tebbel and Keith Jennison write, "they were confined for the most part to reservations in [the] western United States, victims of discriminatory laws enacted by white bigots and of governmental neglect and mismanagement of their affairs."[3]

As to why the defeat of the American Indian was so complete and final, historians point to a number of major factors. First, they say, huge cultural differences divided Indians and whites from the very beginning; and these differences spawned vicious white racism and hatred toward Indians. Second, white greed for Indian land was relentless. Third, the Indians were, for the most part, unable to mount a united front against the whites, which made the white conquest much easier. Fourth, the whites coordinated their seizure of Indian lands with a policy of removing and relocating tribes, a procedure that hastened the destruction of Native American civilization. Fifth, the whites were more numerous and possessed more advanced industry and technology than the Indians. And sixth, some U.S. leaders pursued a policy designed to make Native Americans think and behave like whites and thereby to assimilate them into white society. This attempt to erase the Indians' cultural identity was in effect a form of genocide (elimination of an entire race or people).

Examining these factors in detail, one is forced inevitably toward a single, tragic conclusion. The Native American tribes had no real chance of winning the series of wars and battles they fought with the United States from the late eighteenth to late nineteenth centuries.

This painting by Charles Schreyvogel captures a dramatic moment in a battle between white soldiers and Indian warriors.

For white America, the victory reaped enormous benefits. Among other things, after all, it ensured that the United States would ultimately stretch from the Atlantic to the Pacific. For the Indians, by contrast, their defeat signaled the sad end of an ancient and proud way of life. "Our Indian ways are almost gone," said Buffalo Bird Woman of the Hidatsa tribe in 1926.

Sometimes I find it hard to believe that I ever lived them. My little son grew up in a white man's school. . . . He is a leader among our Hidatsa people, helping teach them to follow the white man's road. . . . But for me, I cannot forget our old ways. . . . Sometimes at evening I sit, looking out on the big Missouri [River]. . . . And tears come to my eyes. Our Indian life, I know, is gone forever.[4]

The Eve of War: Cultural Differences Between Indians and Whites

Chapter 1

Among the major factors driving the wars between the United States and Native American peoples were mutual distrust and hatred. On the part of whites, these feelings often grew into a mean-spirited, even vicious form of racism that represented Indians as barely human. And such attitudes contributed heavily to the defeat and subjugation of the Native American tribes by whites.

The hatred between whites and Indians resulted mainly from misunderstandings stemming from deep-seated cultural differences. In the 1770s, on the eve of the U.S. Indian Wars, these differences were nothing new; nor were violence and bloodshed between the two peoples. All had existed since the English, French, and other Europeans had begun colonizing North America's eastern seaboard in the early 1600s. From the beginning the cultural gap between white Europeans and the indigenous North American tribes had presented a major obstacle to mutual understanding and peace. As University of Wisconsin scholar Peter Nabokov puts it:

> One cannot dream up two more contrary ways of life and systems of belief than those represented by Native American and European societies. The enormous differences in religious values and practices, in the conduct of family and social life, in concepts of property ownership and land use, in traditional attitudes toward work and leisure, made intimacy between Indians and Europeans all too rare. Much of the time they viewed each other as total barbarians.[5]

13

"Savages" Versus "Decent" People

In retrospect, one is struck by the fact that the whites were usually less willing to accept and understand these cultural differences than the Indians were. As long as white settlers did not intrude onto Indian lands or pose a threat to Indian life, the Indians seemed willing to accept, even to help, their strange new neighbors.

The evidence for this tolerant attitude is plain. Contacts between Native Americans and the settlers of Jamestown, Plymouth, and other early white beachheads were at first largely peaceful. For example, the Indians welcomed and helped the English immigrants who established the Jamestown colony on the shore of Chesapeake Bay in Virginia in 1607. The colony started with nine hundred people; but the first winters were harsh, and starvation and disease killed some 750 colonists. The local Indians, members of the Algonquian confederacy of two hundred villages and thirty-two tribes, observed the whites' plight and, out of pity and concern, gave them food and other supplies. For a few short years, the Algonquians and colonists lived together in peace.

English settlers make their initial camp at Jamestown in 1607. There, they encountered the local Indians, who belonged to the Algonquian confederacy of tribes.

After observing that the whites at Jamestown are suffering from starvation, a delegation of local Indians offers them food.

As white populations grew, however, and required more land to sustain themselves, the peace was shattered. Much of the violence grew out of the colonists' arrogance and religious intolerance. First, they believed that they had the right to dominate the Indians and to take their lands because whites were "naturally superior" to non-whites. The whites saw that the Indians did not live in cities with centralized governments and town halls and other public buildings. Further, they did not have banks, schools, churches, and other social institutions the whites took for granted. In white eyes, such disparities with white civilization could only be the result of inferior intelligence and morals. Therefore, went white reasoning, Native Americans must be wild, uncivilized savages. Also, a natural corollary of this line of reasoning was that anyone who was uncivilized and lacked intelligence and morals could not be trusted to deal honestly and fairly with "decent" people. "They have the shapes of men and may be of the human species," wrote Hugh Brackenridge, a white resident of eighteenth-century Pennsylvania, but certainly in their present state they approach nearer the character of Devils; take an Indian, is there any faith in him? . . . Can you trust his word or confide in his promise? When he makes war upon you, when he takes you prisoner . . . will he spare you? [The author concludes that the answer is no.] In this he departs from the law of nature. . . . On this principle are not the whole Indian nations murderers?[6]

Religious Misunderstanding and Intolerance

As for the differences in religious beliefs, the whites were Christians, with strong devotion to the Bible and the existence of one all-powerful and decidedly Christian god. Convinced that theirs was the only true faith, they looked down on Indian religious notions of nature gods and spirits as primitive and childish. It seemed, therefore, not only morally justified for whites to control both Indians and In-

---

 ## "We Never Quarrel About Religion"

Indians and whites often had much difficulty understanding each other's religious views. And whites usually assumed from the outset their own views were right, while Indian ones were wrong. These sad facts are well illustrated in this excerpt from a speech made by a Seneca chief to a Boston missionary in 1805 (quoted in Wilcomb Washburn's *The Indian and the White Man*).

"You say that you are sent to instruct us how to worship the Great Spirit agreeably to his mind, and, if we do not take hold of the religion which you white people teach, we shall be unhappy hereafter. You say that you are right and we are lost. How do you know this to be true? We understand that your religion is written in a book. If it was intended for us as well as you, why has not the Great Spirit given it to us . . . [or] to our forefathers? . . . We only know what you tell us about it. How shall we know what to believe, being so often deceived by the white people? You say there is but one way to worship and serve the Great Spirit. If there is but one religion, why do you white people differ so much about it? Why not all agreed, as you can all read the book? . . . We also have a religion, which was given to our forefathers, and has been handed down to us their children. . . . It teaches us to be thankful for all the favors we receive; to love each other, and to be united. We never quarrel about religion.

An old lithograph shows white missionaries preaching to Indians. Many whites considered it their duty to convert Native Americans to Christianity.

dian lands, but also a divinely inspired duty to convert the "red hea-thens" to Christianity. Typical was this patronizing speech made by a Boston missionary to a chief of the Seneca, a tribe indigenous to northern New York:

> I have come . . . to instruct you how to worship the Great Spirit agreeably to his mind and will, and to preach to you the gospel of his son, Jesus Christ. There is but one religion, and but one way to serve God, and if you do not embrace the

right way, you cannot be happy hereafter. You have never worshipped the Great Spirit in a manner acceptable to him; but have, all your lives, been in great errors and darkness. To endeavor to remove these errors, and open your eyes, so that you might see clearly, is my business with you.[7]

The chief's answer not only revealed how different Indian religious views were, but also used reason and logic to counter the missionary's arrogance and intolerance.

You say that . . . if we do not take hold of the religion which you white people teach, we shall be unhappy hereafter. You say that you are right and we are lost. How do you know this to be true? . . . You say there is but one way to worship and serve the Great Spirit. If there is but one religion, why do you white people differ so much about it? . . . We also have a religion. . . . It teaches us to be thankful for all the favors we receive; to love each other, and to be united. We never quarrel about religion.[8]

In fact, Native Americans did not quarrel over religion because most of them did not see it, as white Europeans did, as a separate institution with its own history, personnel (i.e., priests), and structured beliefs and writings. Instead, writes George Tinker, an expert on Indian religious beliefs,

it has become increasingly clear that those phenomena we call Native American religions were . . . very complex socially and philosophically and are therefore not easily represented or described by means of either popular interpretation . . . or academic analysis. . . . Most adherents to traditional American Indian ways characteristically deny that their people ever engaged in any religion at all. Rather . . . their whole culture and social structure was . . . infused with a spirituality that cannot be separated from the rest of the community's life at any point. . . . Whereas outsiders may identify a single ritual as the "religion" of a particular people, the people themselves will likely see that ceremony as merely an extension of their day-to-day existence, all parts of which . . . should be seen as "religious.". . . Thus, the social structures and cultural traditions of American Indian peoples are infused

All Indians Are Murderers?

The hatred and racism against Indians that developed out of the deep-
seated cultural differences between them and whites is evidenced in this
mean-spirited letter written in the early 1780s by a white settler to the
editor of the then widely read *Freeman's Journal* (quoted in Wilcomb
Washburn's *The Indian and the White Man*).

"Having had the opportunity to know something of the character
of this race of men [the Indians], from the deeds they perpetuate
daily round me, I think it proper to say something on the subject.
. . . They have the shapes of men and may be of the human
species, but certainly in their present state they approach nearer
the character of Devils. Take an Indian, is there any faith in him?
Can you bind him by favors? Can you trust his word or confide in
his promise? When he makes war upon you, when he takes you
prisoner and has you in his power, will he spare you? . . . On this
principle, are not the whole Indian nations murderers? . . . If we
could have any faith in the promises they make, we could suffer
them to live, provided they would only make war amongst themselves, and abandon their hiding or lurking on the pathways of our
citizens . . . and murdering men, women, and children in a de-
fenseless situation."

with a spirituality that cannot be separated from, say, picking
corn or tanning hides, hunting game, or making war.[9]

Clearly, then, Native Americans were just as religious as whites, but
in a very different way, one that the vast majority of whites were unable to comprehend and appreciate.

Differing Views of Land Use

Stark social and economic differences, especially in regards to land
use, also separated Indians and whites. From the Native American
point of view, these differences were acceptable and fitting because
they were part of the natural order of things. "The Great Spirit made
us all," a Pawnee chief named Petalesharo told President James Monroe in 1822.

He made my skin red, and yours white, he placed us on the
earth, and intended that we should live differently from each
other. He made the whites to cultivate the earth, and feed on
domestic animals, but he made us [i.e., Indians] . . . to rove

The Pawnee chief Petalesharo, pictured here, believed that the differences between white and Native American civilizations were the purposeful intent of the Great Spirit.

through uncultivated woods and plains, to feed on wild animals, and to dress with their skins.[10]

The problem was that this simple and tolerant view was completely contrary to that of the whites. "They [the Indians] have by estimation nearly 100,000 acres of land to each man," complained a petition submitted to the government by white settlers in Alabama in 1809. Worse, the natives merely "saunter about" the land "like so many wolves or bears," while the more hardworking whites are prevented "even from enjoying a small corner of this land."[11] This attitude is not surprising. After all, Nabokov points out, the whites defined land

> as a commercial product like sugar or gunpowder. [They] measured it, bought it or stole it, fenced it, tilled or built upon it, with an abandon that horrified the Indians. At the same time the colonists, whose society was founded on

Torn Between Two Cultures

The tremendous cultural rift between Indians and whites had many different aspects and outcomes. One situation that emphasized the differences between the two peoples was when a white person was captured and assimilated by Indians. Here is the story (as told by Benjamin Capps in *The Indians*) of one such captive who was torn between two ways of life with tragic results.

"On a May day in 1836 in northern Texas, a 9-year-old frontier girl was abducted by a raiding band of Comanches, who swooped down on the family home and killed her father. The child was Cynthia Ann Parker, favorite niece of Isaac Parker, rancher, soldier, and legislator. The story of her 25-year captivity and subsequent return is one of the most poignant of all frontier tales. As Cynthia Ann toiled at the work of a Comanche woman, the chief chose her as his bride when she was 18, and she bore three children—two sons . . . and a daughter. . . . For 15 years she cared for her family. . . . Cynthia Ann's return to white society occurred the way she had left it, through a raid. While camped near the Pease River in 1860, her tribe was surprised by a detachment of government Indian hunters. Her husband and her teen-aged sons escaped. . . . Certain that they had found the long-lost lady of the Parker family, the soldiers summoned Isaac Parker. He tried to talk to the blue-eyed woman, but she spoke little English. . . . Finally Parker said, 'Maybe we were wrong. Poor Cynthia Ann.' On hearing the name, the 34-year-old woman remembered it from her childhood. 'Me Cynthia,' she replied simply. Cynthia was welcomed back by the whites, who even voted her a pension and some land. But she never smiled. Several times she stole horses and lit out in quest of her sons. . . . [Eventually her] little girl died from a fever. Devastated by grief, Cynthia Ann starved herself to death."

Cynthia Ann Parker, pictured here, was torn between two cultures.

private ownership and consolidation of personal riches, looked disapprovingly at Indian customs of sharing land in common.[12]

Such disapproval quickly matured into condemnation and open hostility. Moreover, images of Native Americans as uncivilized, savage, untrustworthy, ungodly, and naive and primitive in their views about land use constituted only part of a growing collection of stereotypes perpetrated and widely accepted by whites. White settlers saw themselves as inherently peaceful and benevolent, a race of valiant, hardworking, and God-fearing people attempting to tame a hostile wilderness. In contrast, Indians were pictured as warlike and bloodthirsty by nature; any Indian resistance to white expansion was therefore viewed as hostile, unjustified, treacherous, and murderous.

The First War Between American Colonists and Indians

These attitudes unfortunately made it acceptable among many white colonists to kill Indians and/or confiscate their lands. And responding to such aggression, many Indians developed an almost equal distrust and dislike for whites. The net result was, as noted historian Anthony Wallace says, that "neither side was able to deter violence." Indeed, he writes,

> this had long been a problem for Indian diplomats, whose peace-making efforts were easily subverted by vengeance-seeking warriors; the plaintive excuse was "We cannot control our young men." On the white side, far from eastern centers of power, it was equally difficult to prevent mayhem and murder by violent men. . . . Why belong to a state [the white argument went] that . . . wants to "civilize" the savages rather than drive them off the land, and that abandons you to fight and die alone when the Indians go on the warpath?[13]

The same basic scenario of cultural differences leading first to misunderstanding between whites and Indians, then to violence between them, and finally to the Indians' disastrous defeat was repeated time and again as white civilization marched westward. The events of the very first Indian war in the American colonies established a pattern followed later by the new nation that emerged from those colonies. The setting was Jamestown, where relations between the

*This early nineteenth-century painting captures the deteriorating
relationship between the English settlers at Jamestown and the local
Indians.*

local Algonquians and whites had initially been friendly. In time the
colonists saw that there was an expanding market in Europe for the
tobacco the Indians had taught them to grow in Virginia. To grow
more tobacco required more land. And the colonists had no qualms
about taking over Indian lands for this purpose. Without asking permission, white farmers chopped down forests and planted their crops
in areas where the Algonquians had hunted and fished for centuries.

After the land had been stolen, some Algonquians wanted to retaliate by attacking the white settlement. But the leading chief,
Wahunsenacawh, whom the whites called Powhatan, wanted to
maintain the peace, and he convinced his people to refrain from
fighting. He believed that future trade with the whites would benefit
his people. Also, he assumed that the colonists would never need
more than a few thousand acres to grow their tobacco. In his view,
such a small amount of land did not seem worth dying for, and he
managed to maintain peace with the whites until his death in 1618.

But not long after Powhatan's passing, it became clear to his people that the whites were not satisfied with a mere few thousand acres.
As the Jamestown colonists continued to grab more Indian land,

The Algonquian chief Powhatan, depicted here, wanted to maintain peace between his people and the inhabitants of Jamestown. But after his death war ensued.

those Algonquian leaders who had earlier clamored for war now began to set tribal policy. The most influential of these men was Opechancanough, Powhatan's brother. In the spring of 1622, the new chief led an attack on some of Jamestown's outlying settlements and killed about 350 whites.

Not surprisingly, the colonists then retaliated. But they were not content simply to fight and win a battle to teach the Indians a lesson. Instead, the colonists launched a campaign of extermination against the Algonquians. Year after year they raided Indian villages, massacred all men, women, and children, and burned all crops. Eventually, after more than twenty years of bloodshed, the colonists captured and shot Opechancanough. By this time there were only about a thousand Algonquians left; the whites forced them to live on a small allotment of land, in effect creating one of the first Indian reservations.

To Tame a Continent

During the century or so that followed, many similar confrontations between whites and Indians occurred in the American colonies. And all of these further damaged white-Indian relations, in addition to causing much bloodshed and misery on both sides. Complicating matters, moreover, in the French and Indian War (1754–63), fought for dominance of eastern North America, some Native Americans took the British side, while others fought for the French. Whichever side a tribe took, its ultimate motive was the same. Indians fought in the war mainly because they believed the whites they backed would later protect native hunting grounds. For a while the British, who won the war, appeared ready to offer such protection. Britain drew

A nineteenth-century reproduction of a scene from the French and Indian War, during which some Indian tribes sided with the British, others with the French.

the Proclamation Line, a boundary running north-south through the Appalachian Mountains and separating Indian land from white settlements. Supposedly, all land west of the mountains would remain permanent Indian territory.

But many colonists came to resent the Proclamation Line, feeling that it restricted what they considered their God-given right to

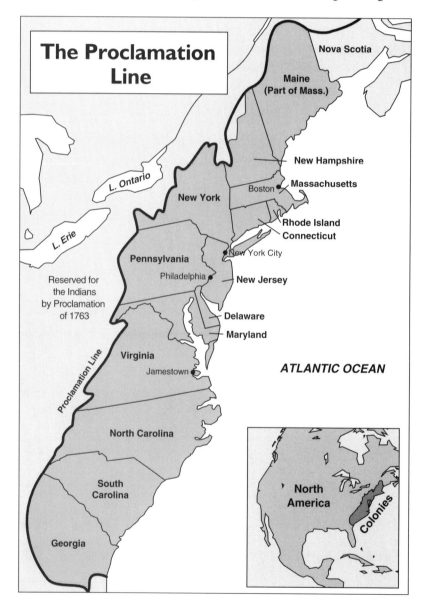

settle anywhere they wanted. When the infant United States emerged from still another confrontation—the American Revolution, fought against Britain—U.S. leaders no longer felt bound by agreements made by Britain; they abolished the Proclamation Line and encouraged white settlement of the Ohio Valley beyond.

As a new nation forged on the principles of freedom and equality, the United States had the chance to make a fresh start with the Indians. However, this positive turn of events never occurred; the fundamental cultural differences between the two sides had bred a century and a half of misunderstanding, hatred, and distrust that was by then too ingrained to be reversed. Moreover, the new nation almost immediately set its sights on subduing the wilderness. All the depredations the Indians had suffered before 1776 would prove but a foretaste of the horrors to come.

Manifest Destiny: White Expansion into Indian Lands

Chapter 2

ERHAPS THE MOST OBVIOUS direct cause of the defeat of Native America by the United States was relentless white expansion westward from the eastern seaboard, accompanied by the confiscation of Indian lands. The process began in earnest in the late 1700s and was more or less complete by about 1890. By that time all of the Native American peoples had been conquered and/or pushed onto reservations or lands that whites viewed as unsuited to their use.

There were two major forces driving this huge and fateful burst of white expansion and land acquisition. In white eyes, both were highly compelling and seemed ample justification for taking Indian lands. The first was the growing concept of "manifest destiny," the idea that white Americans were destined to control all the lands lying between the Atlantic and Pacific Oceans. The other justification was the marked difference in the ways the two races viewed land ownership and use. The whites observed that Native Americans did not create clearly marked property boundaries and did not develop the land the way Europeans traditionally did. To white settlers, that seemed to suggest that the Indians had no compelling claim to the land they lived on; therefore, they did not own it. And if they did not own it, someone else was justified in laying claim to it.

In spite of the fact that most whites felt this way, the U.S. government usually attempted to create the impression that it was buying or trading for Indian lands in a legal, above-the-board manner. The instrument of this process was the Indian treaty. Between 1778 and 1868, the United States negotiated 374 treaties with various tribes. Between 1853 and 1857 alone, Congress ratified fifty-two treaties under which the U.S. "bought" some 157 million acres of Indian lands in Idaho, Oregon, and Washington. In reality, however, these treaties were mostly a pretense for outright land seizure. The bottom line is that many of the treaties were fraudulently negotiated and/or some of their provisions were never fully honored. The treaties turned out to be a mixed blessing for the U.S. On the one hand, such deals allowed the nation to fulfill its manifest destiny; on the other, they left an enduring stain on the country's honor.

Destiny of the "Superior" Race

Ironically, the feelings that initially fueled the concept of manifest destiny were based on the supposition that white Americans were the most "honorable" people in the world. Such feelings of white American superiority had begun to develop during late colonial times. And they increased significantly in the early years of the new nation, which the U.S. founding fathers described as blessed by God. It seemed only natural that a superior people placed by God on the edge of an enormous fertile expanse of undeveloped land should move into and develop that land the way they saw fit.

Several years passed, however, before this concept of divinely ordained white expansion received a formal, popular name and it became

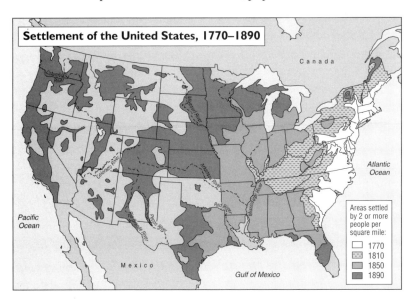

Settlement of the United States, 1770–1890

A white colonial leader reads a list of peace terms to his Native American counterparts.

fashionable to admit publicly that an idea so blatantly arrogant and racist did in fact drive U.S. policy. The term was coined and the policy spelled out in 1845 by the editor of the popular *Democratic Review*, John O'Sullivan. He suggested that God had created the vast lands of the American frontier specifically for the use of the citizens of the United States. "Our manifest destiny," he exclaimed, is "to overspread the continent allotted by Providence [God's will] for the free development of our expanding millions."[14]

The term "manifest destiny" immediately caught on. Most of those who embraced its central theme assumed that since God intended the United States to control the continent, there must be something special about Americans and their nation. This notion was summarized in 1846 in another popular publication, the *New Englander*, which asserted that the U.S.

> sprang from the noblest stock on earth's face, either of past or present times—a stock the most intellectual, as well as moral, and a stock which in physical qualities had

at the time the nation was founded, and yet has, no equal. The very best of the nation of this best stock, founded the United States. . . . From the earliest period of the country to this day, the noble stock that first came to these shores has been widening and strengthening in its principles, and though modified by the thousand other causes that must be at work in so large a people and one so situated, it is destined to perpetuate . . . its wisdom and worth to the latest generation. . . . The government of these United States is believed by the far-judging of the whole world to be the

This famous painting by John Gast, titled "Manifest Destiny," captured white American feelings that their westward expansion was divinely inspired.

"The White Man Wants Our Land"

This is an excerpt from an 1838 Native American speech protesting the relentless white expansion into Indian lands, what would later come to be called "manifest destiny." The reasoned, eloquent words (quoted in Annette Rosenstiel's *Red and White*) are those of Maris Bryant Pierce, of the Seneca tribe, made to the members of a Baptist church in Buffalo, New York.

"In the first place, the white man wants our land; in the next place, it is said that the offer for it is liberal. . . . The fact that the whites want our land imposes no obligation on us to sell it, nor does it hold forth an inducement to do so, unless it leads them to offer us a price equal in value to us. We neither know nor feel any debt of gratitude which we owe to them, in consequence of their 'loving kindness or tender mercies' toward us, that should cause us to make a sacrifice of our property or our interest, to their wonted avarice [greed] which . . . cries give, give, and is never sated [satisfied]. . . . Since in us is vested a perfect title to the land, I know not why we may not, when we wish, dispose of it at such prices as we may see fit. . . . [White] population is with rapid strides going beyond the Mississippi. . . . And in the process of time, will not our territory there be as subject to the wants of the whites as that which we now occupy is?"

model government in the earth; and to be thought therefore worthy at least of being held up before other nations . . . as a sort of guide, by which they may direct their own steps in the cause of general progression of the human race.[15]

Though this tract seemed on the surface to be mainly a political glorification of the American system of government, the frequent use of the term "stock" (physical, moral, and so on) betrayed its underlying racist content. It and other pieces like it tended to reinforce a belief then widely held in the United States, namely, that white Protestant Americans were superior to other peoples. Such misguided notions provided a convenient justification for pushing aside the Native American tribes that stood in the way of white expansion. According to this view, it was only natural and right that such "inferior" peoples give way to their white "betters." As a Massachusetts missionary Timothy Flint argued in 1833:

In the unchangeable order of things, two such races cannot exist together, each preserving its coordinate identity. Either this great continent, in the order of Providence, shall have remained in the occupancy of half a million savages, engaged in everlasting conflicts of their peculiar warfare with each other, or it must have become, as it has, the domain of civilized millions.[16]

Who Owned the Land?

As for the issue of who actually owned the land, whites typically argued that the Indians could not lay claim to land that they merely "roamed over" and "hunted on." Also according to this view, white settlers developed the land by farming it; set up fences, stone walls, and other clearly recognizable boundaries around it; built permanent cities on it; and in general brought to it the fruits of "progress" and "civilization." President Theodore Roosevelt, who in regards to Indians was essentially an apologist for white appropriation of their lands, later summed up the white view this way:

White settlers clear a section of forest to create a farm. Whites typically believed that working the land this way gave them ownership rights over it.

It cannot be too often insisted that they [the Indians] did not own the land; or, at least, that their ownership was merely such as that claimed often by our own white hunters. . . . To recognize the Indian ownership of the limitless prairies and forests of this continent—that is, to consider the dozen squalid savages who hunted at long intervals over a territory of a thousand square miles as owning it outright—necessarily implies a similar recognition of the claims of every white hunter, squatter, horse-thief, or wandering cattle-man. . . . The different tribes have always been utterly unable to define their own boundaries. . . . The tribes were warlike and bloodthirsty, jealous of each other and of the whites; they claimed the land for their hunting grounds, but their claims all conflicted with one another; their knowledge of their own boundaries was so indefinite that they were always willing, for inadequate compensation, to sell land to which they had merely the vaguest title [of ownership]; and yet, when once they had received the goods, were generally reluctant to make over [develop] what they could.[17]

By contrast, most Indians believed that the Great Spirit had not created the land to be developed by specific races, tribes, or individuals. Instead, the land had been provided by Providence for all people to use when and as needed. Furthermore, God had placed no artificial boundaries or other markers on the land. Why, then, should humans presume to do so? The earth "should be left as it was," said the famous Nez Percé leader, Chief Joseph. "The country was made without lines of demarcation, and it is no man's business to divide it." Similarly, it was not people's business to buy and sell land in the exacting manner that whites did. "The one who has the right to dispose of it," Chief Joseph argued, "is the one who has created it."[18] In other words, God was the true owner of all land and only He could decide how and by whom it was used.

Indeed, differing concepts of and disputes over land ownership and use rested at the heart of the struggles between white and Native Americans. A core cause of conflicts between the two peoples ever since the onset of European settlement of North America, this dispute greatly intensified in the late 1700s, when the infant United States began fulfilling its manifest destiny and pushing westward. The future of the continent now depended on the answers to two basic questions. First, could whites and Indians find a way to coexist on the American frontier? Second, assuming that they could not coexist, could the Indians stop the inevitable and relentless white advance?

No One Owns the Land

Many American Indians felt that no one could own or dispose of land except the Creator. This view is presented here by Chief Joseph, of the Nez Percé tribe (whose words are quoted in T. C. McLuhan's *Touch the Earth*).

The great Chief Joseph, pictured here, argued that humans had no right to divide up the land.

"The earth was created by the assistance of the sun, and it should be left as it is. . . . The country was made without lines of demarcation, and it is no man's business to divide it. . . . I see the whites all over the country gaining wealth, and see their desire to give us lands which are worthless. . . . The earth and myself are of one mind. The measure of the land and the measure of our bodies are the same. Say to us if you can say it, that you were sent by the Creative Power to talk to us. Perhaps you think the Creator sent you here to dispose of us as you see fit. If I thought you were sent by the Creator, I might be induced to think you had a right to dispose of me. Do not misunderstand me, but understand me fully with reference to my affection for the land. I never said the land was mine to do with as I chose. The one who has the right to dispose of it is the one who has created it. I claim a right to live on my land, and accord you the privilege to live on yours."

Two Opposing Visions of the Future

Initial attempts by both sides to answer such questions are conveniently summarized in the future visions of the third president, Thomas Jefferson (born in 1743 in the English colony of Virginia), and Tecumseh, a Shawnee chief (born about 1768 near the current site of Springfield, Ohio). Jefferson viewed the western march of white settlers as necessary for the growth and prosperity of the United States. He believed that the country's future would be shaped by independent, hardworking yeoman farmers, who would set an example for other Americans.

Jefferson was well aware that westward settlement would cause land disputes with Native Americans. But he fully accepted the argument that tribal failure to develop the land, using the white definition of such development, negated any Indian claims of ownership. He saw two basic possibilities for the Indians' future. They could either learn to become independent farmers in the white sense and slowly

Thomas Jefferson, the third U.S. president, envisioned a westward march of hardworking, independent white yeoman farmers.

assimilate into white culture, or they could find new lands to live in. Jefferson assumed that because many Indians hunted, fished, and otherwise lived off the land, they could live anywhere; so why not let them move farther west, beyond the Mississippi, to make room for white settlers? In 1803 he wrote to the governor of the Ohio Territory, saying:

> They [the Indians] will in time either incorporate with us as citizens of the United States or remove beyond the Mississippi. The former is certainly the termination of their history most happy for themselves, but, in the whole course of this, it is essential to cultivate their love. As to their fear, we presume that our strength and their weakness is now so visible that they must see that we have only to shut our hand to crush them, and that all our liberalities to them proceed from motives of pure humanity only.[19]

This statement shows that Jefferson, like most other whites of his time, had already concluded that the Indians were a doomed race. Or at least the Indian way of life east of the Mississippi was doomed; the red race, Jefferson sincerely believed, could still save itself by retreating westward. He did not take into account, or perhaps did not care, that the Indians who already lived west of the great river might resent eastern Indians entering their territories. At least, in his view, whites and Indians could thereafter stay out of each other's way and coexist on the same continent in peace. In fact, he more than once expressed what later events proved to be the naive, wholly unrealistic idea that the West was large and bountiful enough to accommodate all, white and red alike, for many generations to come.

Predictably, Tecumseh's view of the future of his race was quite different than Jefferson's. Tecumseh held fast to the Native American view that the Great Spirit had created the land for everyone's use. But he added an important twist, namely, that "everyone" included the various Indian tribes, not white Europeans. The Indians had been there first, he said, and the whites were clearly trespassers. In past ages, he said:

> there was no white man on this continent. It then belonged to red men, children of the same parents, placed on it by the

The Shawnee chief Tecumseh, pictured here, was highly critical of Native Americans who sold their land to the whites without consulting neighboring tribes.

Great Spirit that made them, to keep it, to traverse it, to enjoy its productions, and to fill it with the same race.[20]

Based on this concept, Tecumseh came to the logical and crucial conclusion that no single tribe could sell the land to the whites. Since it belonged to all Indians, all had to agree to such a sale, which otherwise would be illegal. Thus, the Indians must recognize that all earlier treaties were worthless and refuse to accept their provisions. And no further treaties should be negotiated with the whites except by representatives of all the tribes. Tecumseh seemed convinced that the whites' westward expansion could be halted by these legal technicalities. This would, he reasoned, ensure the future security of Native American civilization.

A Long Series of Deceptions and False Hopes

Tecumseh's approach proved too idealistic and unworkable, however. Many tribes continued to make their own individual treaties with the United States, each trusting that its deal was fair and would bring lasting peace between itself and whites. But the reality was that

 ## "We Are Men, Not Children"

It is well known that the United States made many treaties with Native Americans and then later, in its relentless effort to fulfill its "manifest destiny," flagrantly broke most of them. During the negotiations of these agreements, government officials often treated Indian representatives in a paternalistic, patronizing manner. For example, this is an excerpt (quoted in Peter Nabokov's *Native American Testimony*) from a meeting that took place in 1873 between the commissioner of Indian Affairs and two chiefs of the Oto tribe—Stand By and Medicine Horse. The chiefs have just learned that a treaty they signed earlier contains a clause allowing the government to withhold much of the money it owes them for their land.

"Commissioner: The President decided whether to give the money or [else] other things which he considers better for you. I will not take your money away but will spend it so as to do you good. . . .

Stand By: How would these white men feel to have their property used in this way?

Commissioner: If the white men are children and you are their guardian, you can do what you please with their money—provided you do what is good for them.

Medicine Horse: We are not children. We are men. I never thought I would be treated so when I made the treaty.

Commissioner: I have no way of knowing what was said at the time of the making of the treaty, but to read what is written on the paper on which you have put your mark. If this course I propose was injuring you, I should not propose it. But it is for your own good.

Medicine Horse: Father, look at me and not at the table.

Commissioner: I am busy writing. . . .

Medicine Horse: We will not talk anymore now. We will think about it."

the majority of such deals were anything but fair. Often the treaties contained deceptive language or fine print that Native Americans, who were unused to such formal legal documents, did not understand. Many Indian negotiators thought that by signing a treaty they were merely allowing the whites to hunt and fish on or travel across Indian lands. Only later did Indians find out that they had granted the whites "ownership" and dispossessed themselves of their own lands. As the Oglala Sioux leader Red Cloud later complained:

> In 1868, [white] men came out and brought papers. We could not read them, and they did not tell us truly what was in them. . . . When we reached Washington, the Great Father [i.e., the president] . . . showed me that the interpreters had deceived me.[21]

Similar was the experience of Black Hawk, a chief of the Sauk tribe. "I touched the goose quill to the treaty," he said, "not knowing, however, that by that act I consented to give away my village."[22]

A more or less typical pattern of abuse emerged in the government's treaty-making negotiations. First, the fine print of a treaty, so often overlooked by Native American negotiators, frequently demanded that the local Indians move to the least fertile section of the territory they inhabited; or it called for them to vacate the land entirely. Also, Peter Nabokov explains,

> a pervasive [widespread] form of abuse . . . was to rush tribesmen into affixing their X marks . . . to treaty agreements before they had had time to discuss the matter. . . . Often those who approved the treaty were any agreeable Indians the white negotiators could hastily collect for a meeting, or a clan leader who was unauthorized to speak for the entire tribe. . . . Government officials also exploited schisms [divisions] within Indian communities, playing one side against the other. They often neglected to explain that presents lavished upon their Native American guests during treaty negotiations were actually partial payment for lands soon to be gone forever.[23]

The devastating impact of such abuses can be seen clearly, for example, in the very first Indian treaty negotiated by the United States. It was signed by the Delaware in 1778. In return for a native promise to help the new country fight the British, the government pledged to grant the tribe statehood after the conclusion of the Revolutionary War. Instead, this document and seventeen more the tribe later signed stripped the Delaware of their land and forced them to move to Canada, Oklahoma, and other faraway places. The U.S. government perpetrated a series of similar outrages against numerous other tribes in the years that followed.

A handful of American leaders felt guilty for such transgressions. Thomas Jefferson, for instance, called them "a principal source of dishonor to the American character." After defrauding the Indians of their land, he said, "they cannot love us," and he hoped that in time the whites might "recover their esteem" by negotiating more fairly with the natives.[24] This, however, would ultimately prove a false hope.

Tears for Tecumseh: The Lost Cause of Indian Unity

Chapter 3

THROUGHOUT HISTORY A FREQUENT and glaring cause for the downfall of various peoples has been a lack of unity in the face of aggression. In the case of Native Americans, the hundreds of tribes that faced the expanding ambitions of the infant United States failed to create a united front against the white aggressors. Dale Van Every, author of *The Disinherited: The Lost Birthright of the American Indian*, summarizes the problem this way:

> The basic Indian weakness in coping with the ever-growing threat to their existence as a people was from the outset their failure to recognize the community of their interests as a people. They were confronted by an appalling and unmistakable clear and present danger. Their homeland was being overrun by alien invaders bent upon their extermination. Yet, from the days of the first white appearance on the continent to the days when the last flickers of Indian resistance were being extinguished, Indians exhibited no urgent impulse to combine in their common defense. . . . Throughout the period of progressively accelerating white conquest, Indians continued to devote much more energy to their wars upon each other than to efforts to resist the invaders.[25]

Whether or not a pan-Indian (all-Indian) alliance would have succeeded in permanently halting U.S. expansion is questionable. After all, the whites enjoyed other important advantages over the Indians besides unity. Still, a large and lasting alliance of most of the tribes against the common threat would certainly have significantly slowed the white conquest; and even if they had still lost in the end, the Indians might well have been able to negotiate a more equitable peace that allowed them more dignity and autonomy.

As it happened, however, no such large and lasting pan-Indian alliance materialized. Only a handful of Native American leaders truly appreciated the importance of this goal. And only one, the Shawnee chief Tecumseh, dedicated himself heart and soul to achieve it on a grand scale. The fascinating and tragic story of his heroic effort shows how the Indians allowed their greatest potential strength to become their greatest weakness.

One Race Would Have to Give Way

Perhaps what made Tecumseh different from most other Native American leaders was that he fully recognized the cold reality of manifest destiny. The fact that most of the others continued to sign

The ever-diligent Tecumseh, who, more than any other single Indian leader, attempted to create a united Native American front against the whites.

Tecumseh Demands Restoration
of Indian Lands

This is an excerpt (quoted in Edward Spicer's *Short History of the Indians of the United States*) from an 1811 speech made by the Shawnee chief Tecumseh to William Henry Harrison, then governor of the Indiana Territory. The chief warns that the whites' continued failure to return stolen Indian lands will incur the wrath of an alliance of "all the tribes."

"Brother . . . you said that if we could show that the land was sold by people who had no right to sell [it], you would restore it. Those that did sell it did not own it. It was me. These tribes set up a claim, but the tribes with me will not agree with their claim. If the land is not restored to us you will see, when we return to our homes, how it will be settled. We shall have a great council, at which all the tribes will be present, when we shall show to those who sold [the land] that they had no right to the claim that they set up, and we will see what will be done to those chiefs that did sell the land to you. I am not alone in this determination; it is the determination of all the warriors and red people that listen to me. I now wish you to listen to me. If you do not, it will appear as if you wished me to kill all the chiefs that sold you the land. I tell you so because I am authorized by all the tribes to do so. I am the head of them all; I am a warrior, and all the warriors will meet together in two or three moons [i.e., months] from now; then I will call for those chiefs that sold you the land and shall know what to do with them. If you do not restore the land, you will have a hand in killing them."

---

individual treaties with the whites suggests that they did not believe in their hearts that the United States would actually go so far as to completely dispossess all the tribes on the continent.

Indeed, that such a deed was part of U.S. policy was at first denied even by some white leaders. Thomas Jefferson, for instance, did not initially believe that his country should or would go that far. During his first term as president, he still seemed to accept the idea that the United States and most of the Indian peoples living beyond the Appalachians might coexist in peace. In 1801 he sent a commission to negotiate with four major southern tribes—the Cherokee, Creek, Chickasaw, and Choctaw. Among the instructions Jefferson gave the commissioners was the following:

By information lately received, it is evident that the Cherokees have testified much dissatisfaction on hearing that the government was about to request them to cede more land. It is the wish of the president that you should treat the subject with great tenderness, and that you should not press them on any other subjects than those which relate to roads, and settlers thereon. You will impress upon them . . . that the United States have no desire to purchase any of their land, unless they are quite willing to sell; that we are not in want of lands, but only wish to be accommodated with such roads as are necessary to keep up a communication with all parts of the United States, without trespassing on the lands of the red people.[26]

But Jefferson's early vision of U.S.-Indian relations, in which he expressed such well-meaning paternal concern for his "red children," was, in the words of noted historian Stephen Ambrose, "all a pipe dream." One may "as well try to stop an avalanche as to stop the moving frontier,"[27] Ambrose adds. Jefferson himself eventually came to grasp this reality.

And so did Tecumseh. After fighting and trying to negotiate with whites for many years, he came to see that white westward expansion would continue relentlessly and indefinitely. And unlike Jefferson, he

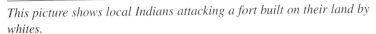

This picture shows local Indians attacking a fort built on their land by whites.

realized early that there was not enough land to accommodate both Indians and whites. One race or the other would have to give way; and there was every reason to believe that the western Indians would suffer the same fate the eastern ones had in colonial days. "Where today are the Pequot?" Tecumseh asked other Indians.

> Where are the Narragansett, the Mohican, the Pocanet, and other powerful [eastern] tribes of our people? They have vanished before the avarice [greed] and oppression of the white man, as snow before the summer sun. . . . Will we let ourselves be destroyed in our turn, without making an effort worthy of our race? Shall we, without a struggle, give up our homes, our lands, bequeathed to us by the Great Spirit? The graves of our dead and everything that is dear and sacred to us? . . . I know you will say with me, Never! Never![28]

"We Are Threatened by a Great Evil"

In time Tecumseh came to the realization that the only way to stop the white tidal wave was for all Indians to unite. And he dreamed of forging one mighty alliance of all the tribes from Canada to the Gulf of Mexico. In an effort to make that dream a reality, in the early 1800s he traveled through the Great Lakes region, then southward through the Ohio Valley and into the Deep South. All along the way, he tried to rally local tribes to his cause. Only a leader of extraordinary vision and talent could have set such a difficult goal and expended such tremendous effort to achieve it. And indeed, it has often been argued that Tecumseh was one of the greatest natural leaders in human history. "A great orator, he could inspire," scholar Carl Waldman points out.

> A brilliant strategist, he was effective in battle; a visionary, he saw what it would take for his people to have an essential role in the future of North America; a man of compassion, he railed against torturing prisoners [a common practice among both Indians and whites at the time]. And he pursued his goals with unflagging energy.[29]

In the early years of the crusade, Tecumseh was accompanied by his brother, Tenskwatawa, who became better known as "the Prophet" because he claimed to have experienced visions. The brothers set up

Tenskwatawa, known as the Prophet, helped his brother, Tecumseh, establish a number of villages in which members of different tribes lived together.

a series of pan-tribal villages, this in itself an incredible achievement considering that most Indian tribes had distinct customs and traditions and did not relish the notion of living together. They also preached that all Indians should stop trading with whites and give up their use of white products. (These included whiskey, for which many Indians eagerly traded, and tools and other forms of white technology.)

Of course, the primary message of Tecumseh, who gradually took over the leadership of the movement from Tenskwatawa, was

Indian unity. Typical of the moving speeches Tecumseh delivered to his fellow Native Americans was the one excerpted here, given to the Osage (who dwelled in what is now eastern Missouri) in 1811:

> [We] are threatened with a great evil; nothing will pacify them [the whites] but the destruction of all the red men. . . . Brothers, the white men want more than our hunting grounds. They wish to kill our warriors. They would even kill our old men, women, and little ones. . . . Brothers, the white men de-

Making the Case for Indian Unity

In 1811 Tecumseh visited many Indian tribes in an attempt to unite them against the growing threat of white westward expansion. The following tract (quoted in Peter Nabokov's *Native American Testimony*) is from the chief's address to the Osage tribe.

"Brothers, we all belong to one family; we are all children of the Great Spirit; we walk in the same path; slake our thirst at the same spring; and now affairs of the greatest concern lead us to smoke the pipe around the same council fire! Brothers, we are friends; we must assist each other to bear our burdens. The blood of many of our fathers and brothers has run like water on the ground, to satisfy the avarice [greed] of the white men. We, ourselves, are threatened with a great evil; nothing will pacify them but the destruction of all the red men. . . . Brothers, the white people are like poisonous serpents. When chilled, they are feeble, and harmless, but invigorate them with warmth, and they sting their benefactors to death. . . . Brothers, the white men want more than our hunting grounds. They wish to kill our warriors. They would even kill our old men, women, and little ones. . . . Brothers, the white men despise and cheat the Indians. They abuse and insult them; they do not think the red men [are] sufficiently good to live. The red men have borne many and great injuries. They ought to suffer them no longer. My people [i.e., the Shawnee] will not. They are determined on vengeance. They have taken up the tomahawk [i.e., gone to war]; they will make it fat with blood. . . . Brothers, my people are brave and numerous. But the white people are too strong for them alone. I wish you to take up the tomahawk with them. If we all unite, we will cause the rivers to stain the great waters with their blood. Brothers, if you do not unite with us, they will first destroy us, and then you will fall an easy prey to them. They have destroyed many nations of red men because they were not united, because they were not friends to each other."

spise and cheat the Indians. They abuse and insult them; they do not think the red men [are] sufficiently good to live. . . . Brothers, my people [i.e., the Shawnee] are brave and numerous. But the white people are too strong for them alone. I wish you to take up the tomahawk with them. . . . Brothers, if you do not unite with us, they will first destroy us, and then you will fall an easy prey to them. They have destroyed many nations of red men because they were not united, because they were not friends to each other. . . . We must be united; we must smoke the same pipe; we must fight each other's battles; and more than all, we must love the Great Spirit. He is for us. He will destroy our enemies, and make his red children happy.[30]

In Tecumseh's view, one obvious key to Indian solidarity was to hold on to and vigorously defend all existing Indian territory. During his travels he witnessed various Indian tribes giving in to white pressure, signing treaties, and selling their lands. One of his bitter responses to such appeasement has fortunately survived. "The only way to stop this evil," he declared,

is for the red men to unite in claiming a common and equal right in the land, as it was at first, and should be now—for it was never divided, but belongs to all. No tribe has the right to sell, even to each other, much less to strangers. . . . *Sell a country! Why not sell the air, the great sea, as well as the earth?* Did not the Great Spirit make them all for the use of his children?[31]

A Lesson from the Past

To convince his fellow Native Americans that there was strength in both unity and continued resolve against the whites, Tecumseh pointed to a series of recent events. In 1790 his tribe, the Shawnee, had formed a temporary alliance with the Miami, Potawatomi, Chippewa, and other tribes under the Miami chief Little Turtle. The goal had been to stop white encroachment into the Ohio Valley and Great Lakes region. That year this unified Indian fighting force had decisively defeated an army of fourteen hundred U.S. troops led by General Josiah Harmar. And about a year later, the Native American alliance under Little Turtle followed up with an even more impressive victory along Ohio's Wabash River. The fierce three-hour battle ended in the most one-sided Indian victory up to that time. The white soldiers, under the command of Revolutionary War hero Arthur St. Clair, counted some 630 killed and 300 wounded, while Indian casualties numbered less than 100.

American general Anthony Wayne prepares his men for battle against Indian forces at Fallen Timbers. Wayne enjoyed a decisive victory.

Embarrassed by these defeats, President George Washington sent General Anthony Wayne with more than three thousand troops to Ohio. In 1794 Wayne built two forts near the site of St. Clair's defeat, and shortly after they were completed, Little Turtle laid siege to them. When he was unable to take the forts, the leader of the Indian coalition decided to give up and make peace. This capitulation angered some of the other Indian leaders, Tecumseh himself among them. They resolved to fight on, but Wayne's forces defeated them at Fallen Timbers (near the western shore of Lake Erie). In Tecumseh's view, this was just a single defeat and a temporary reversal; he was certain that if the alliance remained firm and continued to grow, it could achieve more victories.

However, most of the other Indian leaders disagreed with Tecumseh. Perceiving that they had no other choice, they signed a treaty at Fort Greenville, in Ohio, granting most of Ohio and much of what would become Indiana to the United States. This event, Tecumseh recalled, had marked an important turning point in the history of Indian-white relations. In its wake, thousands of whites began pouring into the region, a human flood that threatened to displace many tribes. Tecumseh had himself refused to sign the treaty and afterward continued his efforts to halt the white advance. The lesson to be learned, he told many Indians in the years that followed, was not only that Indians everywhere should unite, but also that they must remain united and refuse to give up the fight.

The Cold Light of History

To these ends, in 1808 Tecumseh and his brother gathered many warriors and their families in a village stronghold that became known as "Prophet's Town." It stood near the mouth of Tippecanoe Creek, on the Wabash River near the present site of Lafayette, Indiana. The governor of the Indiana Territory, the future president William Henry Harrison, became worried as Tecumseh attracted a growing number of Indian allies to the area. Clearly, Harrison realized, a pan-Indian alliance would pose a potent threat to white settlement of the region. To eliminate what he saw as a menace, the governor waited until Tecumseh had departed on a trip to the South to gather more allies. In November 1811, Harrison led a force of nine hundred American

A nineteenth-century depiction of the Battle of Tippecanoe Creek, in which future president William Henry Harrison established himself as an Indian fighter.

troops to Tippecanoe Creek and attacked Prophet's Town, burning it to the ground and sending the Prophet himself into flight.

This defeat struck a serious blow to Tecumseh's efforts to organize and unite the tribes. But true to his own philosophy and preaching, he did not give up. In fact, shortly afterward an event occurred that gave him renewed hope that the westward expansion of the white settlement could be stopped once and for all. This was the outbreak of the War of 1812, fought between the United States and Britain. The major U.S. goal in this conflict was to expel the British from Canada, while a primary British goal was to keep the U.S. from moving its borders any farther westward. Tecumseh immediately allied himself with the British, believing that the combined Indian and British forces had a real chance of defeating the armies of the United States.

At first this hope seemed justified. After Tecumseh joined forces with Britain's General Isaac Brock, they captured Fort Detroit, on Lake Erie, and Fort Mackinac, on Lake Michigan. These victories inspired many Native American tribes, from the Great Lakes to the Deep South, to join Tecumseh's Indian alliance.

But then Isaac Brock was killed in a minor skirmish. His replacement, General Henry Proctor, was far less talented, and, worse, he was an arrogant individual who did not get along with Tecumseh. After a series of tactical blunders and American victories, Proctor fled Fort Malden, on Lake Erie's western shore, and Tecumseh reluctantly went with him. On October 5, 1813, a U.S. Army troop commanded by Tecumseh's old nemesis, Harrison, caught up with the British and Indians along the Thames River, north of the lake in what today is the Canadian province of Ontario. After a devastating charge by mounted American soldiers, most of the British, including Proctor, fled. But Tecumseh's warriors held their ground, even after they were surrounded. There the great chief and many of his followers died fighting.

In the days that followed, the Shawnee and many other Indians shed tears for the valiant Tecumseh. In the cold light of history, there was indeed even more to cry over than they realized at the time; for

In 1813 Harrison defeated the British and Indians in the battle at the Thames River.

Tecumseh's alliance against the whites died with him, and thereafter the cause of Indian unity was forever lost. This allowed the whites to resume their tried-and-true policy of divide-and-conquer. In a pattern that would be repeated time and again across the continent in later years, some tribes would make peace with the Americans and help them fight other tribes; while those tribes that continued to resist white expansion would be defeated and uprooted one by one.

Removal and Relocation: A Systematic Policy

Chapter 4 of Subjugation

AS THE WARS BETWEEN the United States and the Indian tribes on the eastern frontiers continued, the U.S. government developed one of its most devastating weapons against its Native American opponents. Killing Indians on the battlefield and negotiating unfair treaties with the survivors were obviously major factors in the ongoing defeat of the tribes. But many whites came to the conclusion that this was not enough. On the one hand, a defeated tribe might rise up and attack its white neighbors in the future. On the other, the surviving Indians were clearly in the way of ever-expanding white settlement of the Ohio Valley, Deep South, and other areas. To ensure total and permanent defeat of the tribes, therefore, as well to as make their lands available for white homesteading, they must be removed and forced to live somewhere else.

Statistics Tell the Story

Not surprisingly, U.S. leaders came to see that "somewhere else" as the then unwanted lands lying west of the Mississippi River. Beginning in the 1820s, the U.S. government designated a special region for Indian relocation, which became known, appropriately, as Indian Country (or Indian Territory). At its greatest extent, this area included the lands now encompassed by the states of Oklahoma, Kansas, and Nebraska. According to the U.S. government's new policy, any tribes that stood in the way of white expansion would have to be removed, by force if necessary, and relocated preferably to Indian Country.

At first the U.S. leaders who formulated the official removal policy followed the same naive reasoning expressed by Thomas Jefferson.

55

In his early days as president, Jefferson had assumed that Indians could simply pick up and move practically anywhere and there find some way to live off the land. But for most Indians, the reality of removal was quite different. It caused untold misery and the destruction of entire ways of life, as thousands of people were forced to abandon their ancestral homes and move to distant, unfamiliar territories. And it ensured that those Indians who had been defeated would stay defeated. Dale Van Every provides this moving summary of the policy's terrible impact:

> In the long record of man's inhumanity, exile has wrung moans of anguish from many different peoples. Upon no people could it ever have fallen with a more shattering impact than upon the eastern Indians. The Indian was peculiarly susceptible to every sensory attribute of every natural feature of his surroundings. . . . He knew every marsh, glade, hilltop, rock, spring, creek as only the hunter can know them. . . . He felt himself as much a part of [the land] as the rocks and trees, the animals and birds. His homeland was holy ground,

A Native American tribe reluctantly moves to a new location far from its ancestral lands.

sanctified for him as the resting place of the bones of his an-
cestors and the natural shrine of his religion. He conceived
its waterfalls and ridges, its clouds and mists, its glens and
meadows, to be inhabited by the myriad [large number] of
spirits with whom he held daily communion. It was from this
rain-washed land of forests, streams, and lakes, to which he
was held by the traditions of his forbears . . . that he was to
be driven to the arid, treeless plains of the far west, a deso-
late region then universally known as the Great American
Desert.[32]

Seen in retrospect, this policy of dislocating entire peoples was
probably inevitable. The westward flood of whites driven by "manifest destiny" was, after all, huge in sheer force of numbers. Indeed,
as noted American historian Howard Zinn puts it, "statistics tell the
story." In 1790, he writes,

there were 3,900,000 Americans, and most of them lived
within 50 miles of the Atlantic Ocean. By 1830, there were
13 million Americans, and by 1840, 4,500,000 had crossed
the Appalachian Mountains into the Mississippi Valley—
that huge expanse of land crisscrossed by rivers flowing
into the Mississippi from east and west. In 1820, 120,000
Indians lived east of the Mississippi. By 1844, fewer than
30,000 were left. Most of them had been forced to migrate
westward.[33]

Genesis of the Removal Concept

Although the wholesale removal of the eastern Indians did not begin
in earnest until the 1830s, the genesis of the idea came much earlier.
In fact, Thomas Jefferson, who fancied himself an advocate of fair
and humane treatment of Indians, was the first U.S. president to con-
template a removal program. Jefferson had initially expressed the
view that white Americans should not seek Indian lands unless the
natives wanted to sell them. But the rapid expansion of the frontier,
as well as a huge increase in the number of whites who wanted to settle in it, altered his outlook.

In this regard, the Louisiana Purchase was crucial. This enormous territory, stretching from the Gulf of Mexico in the South to the

The Indian Removal Act

This is an excerpt from the beginning of the text of the Indian Removal Act passed by Congress in 1830 (quoted in Anthony Wallace's *The Long, Bitter Trail*). Despite the use of such benign, fair-sounding phrases as "exchange of lands" and "such tribes . . . as may choose to exchange," in reality the Indians were being forced from their lands with little or no choice in the matter.

"An Act to Provide for an Exchange of Lands with the Indians Residing in any of the States or Territories, and for their Removal West of the River Mississippi. Be it enacted by the Senate and House of Representatives of the United States of America, in Congress assembled, That it shall and may be lawful for the President of the United States to cause so much of any territory belonging to the United States west of the river Mississippi, not included in any state or organized territory, and to which the Indian title has been extinguished, as he may judge necessary, to be divided into a suitable number of districts, for the reception of such tribes or nations of Indians as may choose to exchange the lands where they now reside, and remove there; and to cause each of said districts to be described by natural or artificial marks, as to be easily distinguished from every other."

foothills of the Rocky Mountains in the Northwest, encompassed more than 800,000 square miles. When Jefferson bought it from France in April 1803, he nearly doubled the size of the United States in a single stroke. No American leader had anticipated gaining so much land so quickly. And that sudden gain changed the dynamic of white-Indian relations. It became increasingly clear to American leaders that white settlers would inevitably move onto these lands, displacing the Indians who inhabited them.

At the same time, in Jefferson's view the most logical place for these Indians to go was beyond the Mississippi. In any case, the Indians were given few options. Just before the deal with France went through, Jefferson wrote to William Henry Harrison, predicting that the Indians "will in time either incorporate with us as citizens of the United States, or remove beyond the Mississippi." Jefferson added that any tribe in the region that went to war with the United States would be making a costly mistake. The result, he said, would be "the seizing of the whole country of that tribe, and driving them across the Mississippi, as the only condition of peace."[34]

Despite these sentiments, Jefferson did not implement an official Indian removal program, nor did his immediate successors, James Madison, James Monroe, and John Quincy Adams. This was partly because at first there seemed to be no pressing need for forcible relocation. In the first two decades or so of the nineteenth century, a number of eastern tribes actually migrated westward voluntarily. By 1804, for example, most of the Sac and Fox had left Illinois and Wisconsin for the West; about twelve hundred Choctaw had moved from Mississippi to Texas by 1820; and by the late 1820s, many of the Delaware who had inhabited Indiana emigrated to Missouri, Kansas, and Oklahoma.

Enter Andrew Jackson

Many Indians remained in the Ohio Valley and Deep South, however, among them members of the Cherokee, Creek, Choctaw, Chickasaw, and Seminole tribes. And by the late 1820s, the U.S. government was determined to remove them. The leading U.S. figure in implementing the first official policy of Indian removal was President Andrew Jackson, who had made a name for himself in part through successful military campaigns he had led against Indian tribes. His goal as president

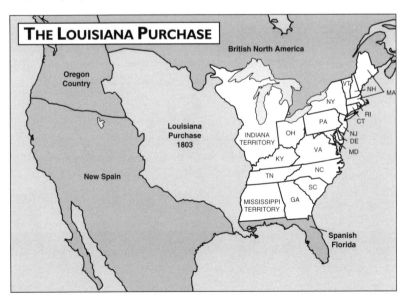

was to create separate living spheres for whites and Indians, motivated in large part by his belief that Indians were inferior and barbaric. Indeed, Zinn is hardly exaggerating when he calls Jackson "the most aggressive enemy of the Indians in early American history."[35]

Jackson's contempt for Indians may have derived from his having grown up among frontier whites who saw Native Americans as

Andrew Jackson, nicknamed "Old Hickory," was one of the most formidable and unrelenting enemies of Native Americans in the early nineteenth century.

*Andrew Jackson meets with a Creek leader shortly before the defeat of the
Creek in 1814. The tribe lost its lands and had to settle on a reservation in
Alabama.*

ever-present threats to their daily existence. In the words of former
Riverside Museum scholar Peter Farb:

> Presidents such as Jefferson, [James] Monroe, and [John
> Quincy] Adams, who came from the east, occasionally dis-
> played some scruples about the treatment the Indian was re-
> ceiving. . . . But President Andrew Jackson had been reared
> on the frontier and he was utterly insensitive to the treatment
> of the Indians. He denounced as an "absurdity" and a "farce"
> that the United States should bother even to negotiate treaties
> with Indians as if they were independent nations with a right
> to their lands. He was completely in sympathy with the pol-
> icy of removal of the Indians to the land west of the Missis-
> sippi. He exerted his influence to make Congress give legal
> sanction to what in our own time . . . would be branded as
> genocide.[36]

The first Indians Jackson dealt with were the Creek, who inhabited what are now Georgia and Alabama. The Creek War of 1813–1814 ended in the total defeat of the tribe and the confiscation of over 23 million acres of former Creek lands by the United States. At first the surviving Creek were forced onto small reservations in Alabama; but later, after Jackson became president, the government forced most of them to move to Indian Country. In 1829 a Creek chief, Speckled Snake, bitterly complained:

> He [the white man] became our Great Father. He loved his red children, but he said: "You must move a little farther, lest by accident I tread on you.". . . Now he says, "The land you live on is not yours. Go beyond the Mississippi; there is game; there you may remain while the grass grows and the rivers run.". . . Brothers, I have listened to a great many talks from our Great Father. But they always began and ended in this—"Get a little farther; you are too near me."[37]

Their World Dismembered

Jackson also fought, defeated, and later relocated other southeastern tribes. He made sure that he had the full force of the law behind him, for in 1830, at his urging, Congress passed the Indian Removal Act. The bill tactfully did not mention the use of force. But the message was clear enough. Any Indians who did not move when told to do so would find themselves without government protection and at the mercy of their white neighbors. And in any case, force *was* ultimately used on numerous occasions.

Among the tribes that resisted removal were the Seminole, who lived in northern Florida. They fiercely and valiantly resisted U.S. troops for more than two decades before being overrun. Between 1835 and 1842, the U.S. government shipped about three thousand Seminole to Indian Country; the remaining two thousand members of the tribe escaped deep into the Florida swamps, where whites could root them out only with great difficulty.

Removal of other tribes, including the Cherokee, Choctaw, and Chickasaw, proceeded much more efficiently, however. Efficiently, that is, from the white point of view, for relocation caused these Indians to endure terrible hardships. Among these was forcing one tribe onto the land of another and thereby provoking war. Such intertribal conflicts had been known well before Jackson's presidency. In 1817, for example, six thousand Cherokee had moved from South Carolina to the Arkansas Territory, then part of Indian Country. The Osage, who already inhabited that region, had seen the newcomers as intruders; the two tribes had gone to war in 1821, and both sides had suffered heavy casualties.

Now, in the wake of the Indian Removal Act, more hardships ensued, not the least of which were the harsh conditions of the journeys themselves. Late in 1831, for instance, some thirteen thousand Choctaw reluctantly headed west. "Marshaled by guards," Van Every writes,

> hustled by agents, harried by contractors, they were being herded on the way to an unknown and unwelcome destination like a flock of sick sheep. . . . The long somber columns of groaning ox wagons, driven herds, and straggling crowds on foot inched on westward through swamps and forests, across rivers, and over hills, in their crawling struggle from the lush lowlands of the Gulf to the arid plains of the west. In a kind of death spasm, one of the last vestiges of the original Indian world was being dismembered and its collapsing

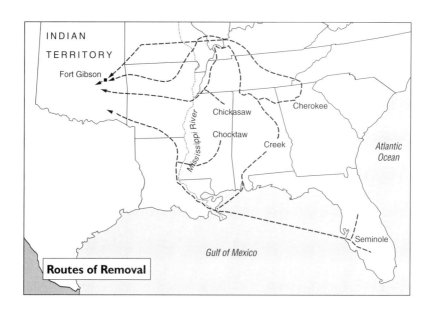

Jackson's Ultimatum
to the Cherokee

This is part of the letter (quoted in John Ehle's *Trail of Tears*) made public on April 7, 1835, by President Andrew Jackson, in which he delivered an ultimatum to the Cherokee in Georgia to vacate their lands.

"My Friends: I have long viewed your condition with great interest. For many years I have been acquainted with your people. . . . Your fathers were well known to me and the regard which I cherished for them has caused me to feel great solicitude for your situation. . . . Listen to me, therefore, as your fathers have listened, while I communicate to you my sentiments on the critical state of your affairs. . . . Most of your young people are uneducated, and are liable to be brought into collision at all times with their white neighbors. Your young men are acquiring habits of intoxication [drunkenness]. With strong passions, and without those habits of restraint which our laws . . . render necessary, they are frequently driven to excesses which must eventually terminate in their ruin. The [wild] game has disappeared among you and you must depend upon agriculture and the mechanical arts for support. And yet, a large portion of your people have acquired little or no property in the soil itself, or in any article of personal property which can be useful to them. How, under these circumstances, can you live in the country you now occupy? Your condition must become worse and worse, and you will ultimately disappear, as so many tribes have done before you. . . . All of this I warned your people when I met them in council eighteen years ago. I then advised them to sell out their possessions east of the Mississippi and to remove to the country west of that river. This advice I have continued to give you . . . down to the present day, and can you now look back and doubt the wisdom of this counsel? . . . Circumstances that cannot be controlled, and which are beyond the reach of human laws, render it impossible that you can flourish in the midst of a civilized community. You have but one remedy within your reach. And that is, to remove to the west and join your countrymen, who are already established there. And the sooner you do this, the sooner you will commence your career of improvement and prosperity. . . . The choice is now before you. May the Great Spirit teach you how to choose. The fate of your women and children, the fate of your people to the remotest generation, depend upon this issue. Deceive yourselves no longer. Do not cherish the belief that you can ever resume your former political situation, while you continue in your present residence."

remnants jammed bodily into an alien new world. Upon this pattern of suffering produced by human mismanagement was superimposed the equal mercilessness of nature. The first winter of the Choctaw migration was the coldest in living memory. A people accustomed to the usual warmth of their deep south homeland, insufficiently provided with clothing and blankets, was benumbed in shelterless camps on frozen ground.[38]

The Trail of Tears

The scene was similar but even more horrific in what was perhaps the most infamous case of Indian removal—that of the Cherokee in Georgia. They refused to move, even after their South Carolinian brethren had done so in 1817. In April 1835 President Jackson delivered what was in effect an ultimatum to the Cherokee then living in the region. "You are now placed in the midst of a white population," he told them.

Most of your young people are uneducated, and are liable to be brought into collision at all times with their white neighbors. Your young men are acquiring habits of intoxication [drunkenness]. With strong passions, and without those habits of restraint which our laws . . . render necessary, they are frequently driven to excesses which must eventually terminate in their ruin. The [wild] game has disappeared among you and you must depend upon agriculture and the mechanical arts for support. And yet, a large portion of your people have acquired little or no property in the soil itself, or in any article of personal property which can be useful to them. How, under these circumstances, can you live in the country you now occupy? Your condition must become worse and worse, and you will ultimately disappear, as so many tribes have done before you. . . . Circumstances that cannot be controlled, and which are beyond the reach of human laws, render it impossible that you can flourish in the midst of a civilized community. You have but one remedy within your reach. And that is, to remove to the west and join your countrymen,

President Martin Van Buren gave the orders for the removal and relocation of the Cherokee, which resulted in the Trail of Tears.

who are already established there. And the sooner you do this, the sooner you will commence your career of improvement and prosperity. . . . The choice is now before you. May the Great Spirit teach you how to choose.[39]

A few of the Cherokee living in Georgia heeded this warning and headed west. But many did not, and this prompted Jackson's successor in the White House, Martin Van Buren, to take drastic action. In May 1838, Van Buren ordered seven thousand U.S. troops and Georgia state militia to remove the Cherokee by whatever means necessary. Soldiers quietly surrounded Cherokee homes, then surprised and dragged away the occupants, after which crowds of whites looted and burned the empty houses. Within a week the troops rounded up over seventeen thousand Cherokee and began transporting them west. In this forced march, which came to be known as the "Trail of Tears," dozens of Indians died of starvation, exposure, or illness each day. A white witness later recalled:

> Many of the aged Indians were suffering extremely from the fatigue of the journey. . . . Several were then quite ill. . . . The sick and the feeble were carried in wagons. . . . Even aged females, apparently nearly ready to drop into the grave, were traveling with heavy burdens attached to the back—on the

sometimes frozen ground, and sometimes muddy streets, with no covering for the feet except what nature had given them. . . . They buried fourteen or fifteen [Cherokee] at every stopping place.[40]

In all, more than four thousand Cherokee died before the tribe reached its destination in Indian Country in 1839.

By the early 1840s, the process of Indian removal in the East was almost complete. Some sixty thousand members of various tribes had been uprooted and relocated west of the Mississippi. Of these, about fifteen thousand had died along the way. In Georgia some whites boasted publicly that no Indians remained on their soil, except those in jails. Meanwhile, after seeing to the removal of the Cherokee, President Van Buren told Congress:

It affords me sincere pleasure to apprise the Congress of the entire removal of the Cherokee Nation of Indians to their new homes west of the Mississippi. . . . Their removal has been principally under the conduct of their own chiefs, and they have emigrated without any apparent reluctance.[41]

This renowned painting by Robert Lindneux depicts a tribe on the move toward Indian Country.

An Eyewitness to the Terrible Truth

On January 26, 1839, a Maine resident who had witnessed the Cherokee removal while traveling in the South published an account in the *New York Observer* (excerpted here from Grant Foreman's *Indian Removal*).

"On Tuesday evening we fell in with a detachment of the poor Cherokee Indians . . . about eleven hundred Indians. . . . With their canvas for a shield from the inclemency of the weather, and the cold wet ground for a resting place, after the fatigue of the day, they spent the night. . . . Many of the aged Indians were suffering extremely from the fatigue of the journey. . . . Several were then quite ill, and one aged man . . . was then in the last struggles of death. . . . The sick and feeble were carried in wagons. . . . Even aged females, apparently nearly ready to drop into the grave, were traveling with heavy burdens attached to the back—on the sometimes frozen ground, and sometimes muddy streets, with no covering for the feet except what nature had given them. . . . We learned from the inhabitants on the road where the Indians passed that they buried fourteen or fifteen [Cherokee] at every stopping place, and they make a journey of ten miles per day only on average. . . . The Indians as a whole carry on their countenances [faces] everything but the appearance of happiness. Some carry a downcast, dejected look bordering on the appearance of despair; others a wild, frantic appearance. . . . When I read in the president's message that he was happy to inform the Senate that the Cherokees were peaceably and without reluctance removed . . . I wished the president could have been there that very day . . . and have seen the comfort and the willingness with which the Cherokees were making their journey."

The Cherokee had indeed been removed to their "new homes" beyond the Mississippi, yet even as they settled as best as they could into their new lives in Indian Country, the refugees were not freed from the need to "get a little farther" from the whites, as Chief Speckled Snake had so memorably put it. Soon they and all of the other native inhabitants of the American West would face the continued onrush of white civilization as it spread across the mighty Mississippi in its headlong flight to the Pacific.

White Logistical Advantages: The Conquest of the Western Indians

Chapter 5

To those in the military, "logistics" refers to the effective acquisition, maintenance, and transportation of soldiers, weapons, and supplies. A combatant who has a significant logistical advantage over his opponent is obviously more likely to win the war. And this was unquestionably the situation that existed in the mid–nineteenth century between the U.S. Army and the Native American tribes that still stood in the way of white expansion. The Indians were vastly fewer in number; overall their weapons were not as effective; and they lacked the kind of industrial capability that allowed the whites to produce and move war personnel and supplies. Under these conditions, the cause of the tribes that faced the U.S. Army in the American West was ultimately hopeless. "Neither stealthy ambushes nor full-scale assaults," says Peter Nabokov,

> could stem the unending stream of white reinforcements. In the end, the Indian was simply outnumbered as well as outarmed. Warfare against the whites was at best only a holding action. Native fighting prowess was judged finally by how long a tribe could prolong its retreat or delay its surrender.[42]

Muskets Versus Bows and Arrows

Timing was crucial in terms of assuring victory for the whites over the Indians. The fact is that the white logistical advantage had not been nearly so large in earlier eras. In colonial times and the early decades of the United States, white settlements had been much fewer in number and confined to the eastern seaboard. Consequently, the numbers of settlers had been considerably smaller; and the number

69

of soldiers they could field against the Indians had also been proportionally smaller.

As for weapons, colonial whites mainly used European muskets (or flintlocks), primitive firearms that had to be laboriously reloaded after each shot. These were somewhat but not overwhelmingly superior to the bows and arrows used by the Indians, especially those mounted on horseback. According to scholar Benjamin Capps:

> The early . . . flintlock guns were clumsy to load and fire from horseback. The fact was that a bowman had all the advantage in rate of fire, being able to get off 20 arrows to the musketman's one ball. A frontiersman testified that he had "as soon be shot at with a musket at the distance of one hundred yards, as by one of these Indians with his bow and arrow."[43]

The whites did have the advantage of possessing more muskets than the Indians, as well as the technical facilities to keep producing more. But for the most part, the Indians were able to counter this

---

The early differences between white and Indian weapons are apparent in this old woodcut, in which the Indians wield bows and the whites flintlocks.

Members of a Native American tribe purchase guns from a French trader.

marginal advantage in two ways. First, many tribes eagerly traded
with the British, French, or other European groups to acquire muskets for themselves. (This also gave various tribes a temporary advantage that allowed them to defeat their neighbors. "A tribe with
guns could win against one without them," says Capps, "because of
the noise, smoke, surprise, and effectiveness of the new weapon
when it found its target."[44])

The second way the Indians countered the whites' muskets was
to utilize, often extremely effectively, their familiarity with the local
terrain. Often their battlefield successes were the result of hit-and-
run guerrilla tactics in which they attacked, then retreated into the
bush, then attacked again when the enemy was off guard. The noted
Sauk chief Black Hawk had occasion to see some of the fighting between Americans and British during the War of 1812. Plainly, he was
flabbergasted to see long lines of soldiers marching at each other in
the open, completely vulnerable to volleys of musket and cannon
fire. "Instead of stealing upon each other," he later remarked,

and taking every advantage to kill the enemy and save their own people . . . they march out, in open daylight, and fight, regardless of the number of warriors they may lose! After the battle is over, they retire to feast, and drink wine, as if nothing happened; after which, they make a statement in writing, of what they have done—each party claiming the victory![45]

An Increase in White Advantages

The situation steadily changed, however, as the new country expanded in size and settlers moved relentlessly westward. By 1820 the United States had a population of approximately 10 million, as compared to probably fewer than half a million Indians living in or west of the Ohio Valley. As time went on, of course, the disparity between these figures became ever larger. Also, the country's army became steadily larger and better organized; there were more soldiers, more horses and wagons to carry them (as well as the system of railroads that expanded westward during the nineteenth century), and better communications, including the telegraph.

Most telling of all, the whites developed much more effective firepower. The old muskets steadily gave way to repeating rifles (i.e., ones that could be fired repeatedly without reloading). Among these were the Spencer and Springfield rifles, the latter of which was particularly devastating. As American historian Alan Axelrod points out, the Springfield's

> 3,500-yard range was about twice that of the Spencer. This was of great significance because it also outdistanced Indian weapons, bows and arrows as well as muskets, sometimes making it difficult or impossible for Indians to make effective attacks.[46]

In addition, the whites developed the Gatling gun, which had a cluster of ten barrels that a soldier turned with a crank, discharging the barrels in succession. In theory, it could fire four hundred rounds per minute; however, because of certain mechanical drawbacks it rarely performed this well. Nevertheless, those army units equipped with Gatling guns had a clear advantage over the Indians they encountered. The same can be said for the army's primary artillery piece. It was a twelve-pound howitzer that could fire two shells per

The Sioux Tribes of the Great Plains

Among the many Native American Plains tribes overrun or displaced by the whites were those collectively called the Sioux, who played a major role in the great Indian victory over Custer at the Little Bighorn. The Sioux made up one of the largest of the American Indian nations. The name "Sioux" is an abbreviation used by whites for Nadouessioux, the name given them by their traditional enemies, the Chippewa of Minnesota. The two peoples fought each other in the late 1600s and early 1700s until most of the Sioux migrated farther west onto the Great Plains. The majority of Plains Sioux made their living as seminomadic hunters, following herds of buffalo and antelope across the prairies.

There were many different Sioux tribes, subtribes, and bands. The Sioux, or Dakota, Nation consisted of seven major tribes: the Mdewakanton, Wahpeton, Wahpekute, Sisseton, Yanton, Yanktonai, and Lakota, also known as the Teton. Each of these tribes had several subtribes. For example, the Lakota, the tribe living farthest west, itself had seven subdivisions. These were the Oglala, or "Those Who Scatter Their Own"; the Brule, or "Burnt Thighs"; the Miniconjou, or "Those Who Plant by the Stream"; the San Arcs, or "Those Without Bows"; the Oohenonpa, or "Two Kettles"; the Sihasapa, or "Blackfoot"; and the Hunkpapa, or "Those Who Camp by the Entrance." These different groups maintained a loose unity by attending large tribal meetings every summer. There they participated in celebrations, exchanged news, traded horses and other goods, and made decisions affecting the entire tribe. Other American Indian tribes had similar subdivisions, although few were as diverse and complex as those of the Sioux.

A horse race among Sioux warriors during a yearly meeting of the various Sioux tribes.

In this 1874 photo, units of U.S. Army cavalry and artillery, under the command of General George Armstrong Custer, move westward into the Black Hills of South Dakota.

minute, each with an effective range of well over nine hundred yards. Like the muskets used in the past, the howitzers were effective not so much because of the casualties they inflicted, but because of their novelty. "Frontier artillery troops were not known for their accuracy," Axelrod says, "but howitzers often served to drive off—or frighten off—attacks even by superior numbers of Indians."[47]

In comparison, the Indians had no heavy industry to produce guns and artillery of their own. In fact, before and in some cases even after contact with white civilization, Native Americans lacked many aspects of advanced technology that white Europeans possessed, placing them at a distinct disadvantage. University of Oklahoma scholar Arrell Gibson explains:

> Native Americans lacked several basic items that would have enhanced their technology, made their dominion over the land less fragile, and made them more of a match for the Europeans. First, they lacked the wheel . . . [which] limited their access to labor saving devices such as the pulley. . . . [Also] they had no knowledge of metallurgy other than ham-

mering sheet copper into tools and gold and silver into orna-
ments. . . . Their lack of large domesticated animals and their
failure to apply water power to grinding grain and other bur-
densome tasks made Indians unduly dependent upon human
muscle power. And their limited metallurgical knowledge restricted weapon and tool materials to stone, wood, bone,
antler, and hammered copper, no match for the iron tools,
weapons, and cooking utensils of the Europeans.[48]

As in the case of muskets, Native Americans acquired various aspects of white technology through trade or capture. But without an
industrial base of their own to produce these items themselves, they
fell further and further behind.

Quicker, Colder, and More Brutal

By the 1850s and 1860s, therefore, when white civilization began to
push its way into the American West, the Indians of the plains and
southwestern deserts found themselves severely outnumbered and
outgunned. As a result, white conquest of the western half of the continent was much quicker and in some ways colder and more brutal
than that of the eastern half. White settlers were more brazen than ever
before in moving into and taking Indian lands. And this was partly because they were more confident than ever in their numbers, industrial
base and technical advantages, and, most of all, their soldiers,—who,
in Indian eyes, kept coming and coming in a seemingly never-ending
stream.

A brief overview of these western conflicts illustrates how the
whites applied these logistical advantages with chilling effectiveness.
The wars in question followed more or less the same pattern as those
that had occurred earlier east of the Mississippi. The lure of land to
farm and develop brought a steady stream of white settlers into the
western plains and the Northwest. And other lures—gold and other
mineral wealth and natural resources—induced many whites to move
onto Indian lands in the Dakotas, the southwestern desert regions,
and California. As the whites moved westward, the U.S. Army often
paved the way by building forts along the frontier. These, along with
new towns that white settlers built, became supply bases for further
bursts of white settlement.

In most areas the Indians at first resisted, at times heroically. But invariably, inferior numbers and weaponry, coupled with lack of unity, brought defeat and consignment to reservations, largely in remote unproductive areas. In the 1850s, for instance, the U.S. Army clashed with the Yakima, Walla Walla, and Cayuse tribes in the Oregon Territory (now the states of Oregon and Washington); the Apache and Ute in the New Mexico Territory (now New Mexico and Arizona); and the Lakota Sioux, Cheyenne, and Comanche on the Great Plains. Then, in the early 1860s, war continued with the Apache and engulfed another large southwestern tribe—the Navajo. After the Navajo were defeated in 1864, the army forced some thirty-five hun-

 Frontier Forts Were a Key to the Army's Success

One of the U.S. Army's keys to success in its steady conquest of the western Indians was its network of frontier forts. These structures in the wilderness were the outposts and symbols of the rapidly expanding white civilization, as well as crucial logistical facilities. The forts had several purposes, the most obvious being to provide the soldiers protection from Indians and other enemies. Typically, in times of danger, civilian settlers from the countryside surrounding a fort also sought safety within its walls. Forts were also used as supply bases and operational centers from which to launch military actions against the Indians. In addition, they served as permanent housing facilities for soldiers assigned to specific regions.

Structurally, most such forts consisted of a high enclosed wall made of stone or wood, which protected the buildings and people inside. Wooden versions were known as stockades. Sometimes, for extra protection, the soldiers dug a wide ditch (moat) around the stockade. Only occasionally were the moats around North American forts filled with water. Walkways along the top of the outer wall provided positions from which defenders could fire at approaching enemies. Soldiers could also fire through small holes cut in the walls.

Inside a fort were quarters for the base commander and his troops. There was also a jail to hold captured prisoners, a blacksmith's shop, and storage facilities for supplies. Most frontier forts had trading posts used by local settlers as well as the soldiers. Thus, these forts often became busy trading and meeting places attracting people from dozens or even hundreds of miles away. In time, towns grew up around most forts, and some of these towns eventually became important cities, among them Fort Detroit in Michigan and Fort Omaha in Nebraska.

U.S. cavalrymen massacre a group of Indians. Though the American press often played up Indian massacres of whites, white massacres of Indians were far more common.

dred members of the tribe to march (in what came to be called the "Long Walk") to a relocation camp in eastern New Mexico. This small (forty square miles), dry, and unproductive area was known as "Bosque Redondo." Conditions there became so deplorable that even local white officials called for a government investigation. In 1868 the Navajo were allowed to return to their former lands, now greatly reduced in size, astride the New Mexico–Arizona border, which became their permanent reservation.

Greater Firepower Ignites Massacres

The increasing white logistical advantage not only assured that whites would win more pitched battles against the Indians, but also increased the incidence of out-and-out massacres of Indians by whites. White hatred of Indians was the chief motivation for such massacres, of course. But the fact that the whites were increasingly better armed, while the Indians had fewer and fewer comparable weapons and firepower, gave many whites what they viewed as a sort of license to attack poorly armed or even unarmed Indian bands.

Thus, while many tribes, like the Navajo, suffered defeat, relocation, and/or confinement on reservations, some Indians faced the worse fate of merciless massacre. In such incidents, smaller Indian numbers played a part along with superior white firepower. A typical local tribe had a population of a few hundred, or at best a few thousand, souls, of which only a minority were warriors. And after engaging white forces in battle, the tribe needed time to rest and attempt to regroup. But this always proved a losing proposition, for there was never sufficient time for a tribe to regain its strength before the next wave of white settlers appeared. Moreover, it was during these times of rest and regrouping that a tribe was most vulnerable to sudden attack and massacre by whites. Sometimes such massacres occurred even after a group of Indians had signaled its desire to stop fighting and make peace. Cherokee/Creek scholar Tom Holm, of the University of Arizona, describes two incidents of this sort:

> On November 29, 1864, Colonel John M. Chivington led his Third Colorado Cavalry Regiment in an attack on a Cheyenne and Arapaho camp at Sand Creek, a tributary of the Arkansas River in southeastern Colorado. Black Kettle,

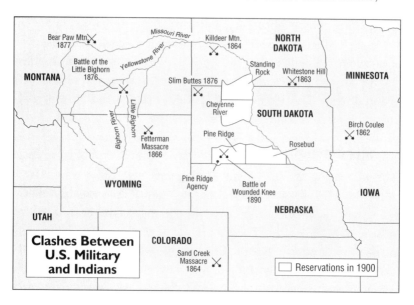

the Cheyenne leader, had just concluded negotiations on a new peace treaty when Chivington's men attacked.

Two hundred Cheyennes died in the onslaught, but, what was worse, Chivington's men dismembered Cheyenne corpses and brought hundreds of body parts back to Denver to be put on display at the local theater. Attacks on tribes by civilian irregulars, however, were even more horrible than those made by regular army troops. In 1871 at Camp Grant, Arizona, for example, a Tucson citizens' group killed and scalped most of the Apache males in the camp, and then raped, murdered, and scalped the women. They took the children to be sold into slavery.[49]

The 1864 Sand Creek Massacre was a horrifyingly clear example of white logistical superiority, combined with out-and-out treachery and cruelty. On the one hand, Black Kettle's people were in the midst of negotiating peace and had no reason to expect an attack. On the other hand, the Indian village had only about five hundred people in it, most of them unarmed women and children. By contrast, Chivington had over seven hundred men, all heavily armed with guns, and also four artillery howitzers. It is difficult to find a more blatant and tragic example of sheer military logistical advantage and overkill in all of the American Indian Wars.

The Most Famous Indian Battle

Despite the whites' increasingly obvious logistical advantage, the remaining Plains tribes stepped up their resistance against white settlers and soldiers. War parties of Sioux, Cheyenne, Arapaho, and other tribes regularly raided white outposts and wagon trains in an effort to slow the encroachment of whites onto Indian lands. In response, the U.S. Army mounted one campaign after another against them. In the late 1860s and on into the 1870s, numerous skirmishes, battles, and massacres took place on the plains as Kiowa, Comanche, Sioux, and others desperately struggled to protect their hunting grounds and way of life.

Occasionally Indians successfully fought against the government forces, but generally such successes resulted from tactical blunders by U.S. commanders, mistakes that counteracted or nullified the superior

A depiction of the battle at Rosebud Creek, in Montana, fought in June 1876, shows U.S. forces engaging the Sioux.

logistics and firepower the whites clearly possessed. The most cele-brated such example of Indians overcoming white logistics thanks to white tactical errors, and probably the most famous of all battles be-tween Indians and whites, was the defeat of George Armstrong Custer and the Seventh Cavalry near the Little Bighorn River (in southern Montana) in 1876. Custer was trying to destroy a temporary alliance of several Plains tribes who had come together in one large encamp-ment near the river. After dividing his forces in an attempt to attack the camp from several angles, his own contingent was surrounded and wiped out by warriors led by Crazy Horse and other chiefs.

The story of the battle has been retold, reconstructed, and de-picted almost endlessly ever since in books and movies. But the ac-tual details of the event are still disputed, partly because none of Custer's 267 men survived to tell the tale. A recently discovered nar-rative by a soldier serving in an army unit that fought on another side of the Indian camp is fascinating and valuable for its insights into Custer's overall campaign; but the author did not actually witness the Seventh Cavalry's demise.[50] Several accounts purportedly by Indians who fought in or observed the battle survived orally and were later written down in English; although some of these accounts are vague or contradictory, a number of others support reconstructions by military historians and are likely accurate. According to a Cheyenne chief, Brave Wolf, "It was hard fighting; very hard all the time. I have been in many hard fights, but never saw such brave men."[51] Crow King, a Sioux, concurred in his own account, which maintains that when Custer's men found themselves surrounded, they dismounted and fought on foot:

> They tried to hold onto their horses, but as we pressed closer they let go their horses. We crowded them toward our main camp and killed them all. They kept in order and fought like brave warriors as long as they had a man left.[52]

It is important to emphasize that this great Indian victory was an unusual exception in the wars between Indians and whites for the American West. It resulted mainly from the fact that Custer unwisely divided his forces, so that his own unit was greatly outnumbered. Also, the large encampment of Indians he encountered was itself highly unusual; never before or after this incident did so many Indian

One of the many paintings depicting the famous battle at the Little Bighorn in 1876, in which Custer was defeated.

Decimation of the Buffalo Herds

One of the most crucial—if unintended—factors in the defeat of the western Plains Indians was white hunters' destruction of the buffalo herds, on which the Indians depended for food and other necessities. Benjamin Capps explains here (from *The Indians*).

"To the Plains Indians, supplying buffalo hides to the white man seemed like good business at first. They always had hunted for their own needs, and merely by killing more buffalo they could obtain guns, tobacco, whiskey and other goods. By the 1840s, they were delivering at least 100,000 hides a year to traders, who shipped the pelts to eastern markets to be sold as lap robes. This increase in hunting by the Indians began to whittle down the total number of buffalo, though there were still an estimated 50 million at mid-century. Soon, however, white men took over the bulk of the hunting and began to kill the animals

A popular magazine shows white buffalo hunters skinning their kill.

with devastating efficiency. Approaching a herd downwind and hiding 200 to 600 yards away behind a rock or shrub, they could pick off the animals without alarming the grazing herd. One hunter might bag 150 buffalo in a day. Then the skinner stripped the animals and pegged the pelts to the ground to dry. The tongues were smoked and sent east to be sold as a delicacy. By the 1860s, the large-scale destruction of the herds by professional hunters . . . was beginning to disrupt the migration patterns of the buffalo. This in turn forced the Plains Indians to move away from their traditional hunting grounds in order to follow the animal that was crucial to their very lives. But no matter where they went, the Indians were almost immediately followed by hunters, soldiers, and pioneers. As Sioux Chief White Cloud lamented, 'Wherever the whites are established, the buffalo is gone, and the red hunters must die of hunger.'"

warriors come together in one place to fight white encroachment. And in its wake, the flood of white settlers and soldiers became larger than ever. Sadly, therefore, in retrospect the Indian victory at the Little Bighorn only serves to highlight the naked truth that in the face of superior white numbers and firepower, the fate of the western Indians was sealed.

Assimilation Versus Self-Identity: The Final Defeat and Its Aftermath

Chapter 6

A S THE INDIAN WARS continued in the American West in the 1860s, 1870s, and 1880s, whites considered the outcome a foregone conclusion. There was no doubt that the Indians were going to lose their struggle to maintain their traditional way of life. Indeed, it was only a matter of time before every tribe was defeated. But some crucial questions remained for white leaders. First, could the final defeat of the Indians be completed without significant further bloodshed? Also, once that defeat had been accomplished, what should be done with the Native American survivors? (Should they continue to be herded onto reservations? And if so, should this be seen as a permanent or only a temporary solution? Should the final goal be to live in peace with them or to eradicate them entirely?)

Even as periodic battles and bloodshed continued in the West, the government formulated what at the time seemed a satisfactory answer to these questions concerning the final fate of the Indians. "At least as early as the administration of Ulysses S. Grant in the mid-1870s," says University of Colorado scholar Ward Churchill, "there was an influential lobby which held that the final eradication of native cultures and population could be achieved more cost-effectively—and with far greater appearance of 'humanitarianism'—through a process of 'assimilation' than by force of arms."[53] The goal of assimilation was to convince and teach the Indians to think and act like whites and thereby, over the course of time, to absorb them into white society.

The U.S. government continued to pursue this policy of assimilation for decades after the last major battle of the Indian Wars, at Wounded Knee in North Dakota in 1890. Clearly, those who im-

84

plemented it reasoned that in time there would no longer be an Indian "problem," since there would no longer be any Indians. No attempt was made to disguise or apologize for the project's stated
goals. One Indian commissioner, Francis Leupp, freely admitted
that the objective was to "kill the Indian, spare the man," so that the
policy of assimilation was in effect "a great pulverizing engine for
breaking up the tribal mass."[54] Fortunately for Native Americans,
the policy was eventually abandoned in favor of allowing them to
keep and perpetuate their identity as a race. Meanwhile the government retained the reservations and insisted that Native Americans
stay on them.

"Your Blood Will Run in Our Veins"

As with so many other white policies regarding Indians, assimilation
had its genesis as a concept long before it was implemented on a wide
scale. In 1808, shortly before leaving the office of president, Thomas
Jefferson received a delegation of Indians in Washington, D.C. The
theme of his message to them was an ultimate union of the races. They
would eventually want to live under white laws, he predicted.

> You will unite yourselves with us, join in our great councils,
> and form one people with us, and we shall all be Americans.

Native Americans attend a white-run blacksmith school in 1882. This was
one way the U.S. government attempted to teach Indians white ways.

You will mix with us by marriage. Your blood will run in our veins, and will spread with us over this great land.[55]

Jefferson had been seriously considering this idea for a long time, as evidenced by this excerpt from a letter to a friend written in 1803:

In truth, the ultimate point of rest and happiness for them [the Indians] is to let our settlements and theirs meet and blend together, to intermix and become one people. Incorporating themselves with us as citizens of the United States,

A Cherokee woman toils on her reservation. Members of many tribes adapted to white ways, including living in houses like the one depicted here.

this is what the natural progress of things will, of course, bring on, and it will be better to promote than to retard it. Surely it will be better for them to be identified with us, and preserved in the occupation of their lands, than be exposed to the many casualties which may endanger them while a separate people.[56]

This sentiment was part of Jefferson's paternalistic attitude toward Native Americans. Like most other whites of his day, he assumed that Indians would be better off adopting white ways; the idea that he might be eradicating an entire race as worthy as his own, along with the moral implications of such an act, clearly did not enter his thinking. Rather, he and other early American leaders seemed honestly to believe that "civilizing" the Indians was for their own good, as in the case of missionaries converting the tribes to Christianity. And many eastern Indians did convert, at least partly, to white ways. Large numbers of the Cherokee in the South, for instance, learned to live in houses and to farm like whites, although this did not stop the government from uprooting them and sending them to Indian Country.

The "Peace Policy"

The attempt to assimilate Indians finally became official government policy during the last two decades of the Indian Wars in the West, when finding a final solution for the Indian "problem" appeared necessary to whites. The matter came to a head with the election of Ulysses S. Grant as president in 1868. Because he was a famous, hardened military man, the U.S. Army hoped and expected him to adopt a tough and, if necessary, brutal approach to the Indian problem. Some of the generals wanted to keep the Indians on their reservations, force them to work at gunpoint, and kill any Indian who dared to set foot off his reservation. This attitude was enunciated in an order issued by General Philip H. Sheridan in June 1869, in which he said:

All Indians when on their proper reservations are under the exclusive control and jurisdiction of their agents [government officials in charge of Indians]. . . . Outside the well-defined limits of their reservations, they are under the original

White Blood Cries for Vengeance

Some whites, especially those who lived in the West near Indian reservations, did not agree with Grant's "Peace Policy," which they saw as giving away too much to the Indians, who did not deserve any mercy. They
felt instead that the army should take charge and "get tough" with the
Indians, as evidenced by this March 1870 editorial in the *Cheyenne Daily
Leader* (quoted in Henry Fritz's *Movement for Indian Assimilation*).

> "A good father is not always indulgent. He discriminates and
> sometimes finds occasion to frown at the wayward children and
> even to use the rod. . . . If it is necessary, let the nation assert its
> rights and its dignity at the mouth of a cannon. Let sniveling
> Quakers give place to bluff soldiers. Let the hell-hounds of the
> wilderness [i.e., the Indians] for once feel the power of the peo-
> ple whom they defy. The blood of thousands of our murdered
> fellow-countrymen cries to heaven for vengeance. And how do
> we avenge them? By an annual tribute of toys and trinkets. By
> annual subsidies of food, clothing, and ammunition. Would that
> the descendants of the Puritans . . . had to live for a few months
> under the shadow of this fulfillment. A short experience of the
> tender mercies of the Sioux or the Comanches would forever
> dissipate the poetical and humane ideas of Indian policy which
> they have contracted from reading Longfellow's 'Hiawatha' [a
> poem that pictures Indians as noble] and contemplating 'picture
> Indians' in their luxurious parlors."

and exclusive jurisdiction of military authority. . . . All Indians . . . who do not immediately remove to their reservations, will be treated as hostile, wherever they may be
found, and particularly if they are near settlements or the
great lines of communication.[57]

However, to the surprise of many, including the generals, Grant
adopted what he thought was a more "humane" approach. Influenced
by the Quakers and other religious and humanitarian groups, in the
early 1870s he issued a series of directives that collectively came to be
known as "Grant's Peace Policy," which was in effect an official recipe
for Indian assimilation. Alan Axelrod summarizes the initiative:

> The object of the Peace Policy was "conquest through kind-
> ness" and emphasized civilian control of the Indian Bureau.
> The Grant administration sought the counsel of church
> groups, especially the Quakers, in nominating Indian agents

and superintendents. A Board of Indian Commissioners was formed, consisting of philanthropists [people who give money to charitable causes] who served without pay. Their mission was to oversee the disbursement of treaty appropriations [distribution of money the government owed Indians for "buying" their lands], which had always been subject to inefficiencies, profiteering, and corruption. The Peace Policy also aimed at ending the traditional treaty system, by which Indian tribes were viewed as "domestic dependent nations" with which the United States had to negotiate as if dealing with sovereign foreign powers. Indians were to be concentrated on reservations, where they would be educated, Christianized, and taught to become self-supporting farmers.[58]

President Ulysses S. Grant initiated what came to be known as his Peace Policy, which was actually an attempt to assimilate Indians into white civilization.

This policy aimed at eventually subdividing, or "allotting," the reservations into individual homesteads. At some unspecified time in the future, planners hoped, the Indian homesteaders would give up their tribal allegiances and more or less blend into American society. White leaders gave little or no thought to the potential destructive effects and moral implications of simply eliminating entire cultures to make way for their own.

Native American reactions to the so-called Peace Policy were predictable. Typically, they echoed the words of a Cherokee named Corn Tassel, who had lived two generations before. "Much has been advanced on the want of what you term civilization among the Indians," he said.

> And many proposals have been made to us to adopt your laws, your religion, your manners, and your customs. But we confess that we do not yet see the propriety or practicability of such a reformation. . . . You say: Why do not the Indians till the ground and live as we do? May we not, with equal propriety, ask, Why the white people do not hunt and live as we do? . . . The great God of Nature has placed us in different situations. It is true that he has endowed you with many

In Montana in 1914, a Blackfoot Indian plows his small plot of land. Though many Native Americans adopted white ways, most were not fully integrated into white society.

The Cheyenne's Failed
Bid for Freedom

Following the Indian victory over Custer in 1876, many white Americans clamored for revenge and called on the U.S. Army to retaliate. Responding to this call, General George Crook and Colonel Nelson A. Miles led a major campaign against the Cheyenne during the winter of 1876–1877. The soldiers defeated the Indians in a number of battles. And eventually the Cheyenne, led by Chief Dull Knife, saw no choice but surrender. They expected to be sent to the Sioux reservation near their traditional hunting grounds, but the army sent them to Indian Country instead.

The Cheyenne found life in Indian Country unbearable. The land was nearly impossible to farm, and the government failed to furnish the supplies it had promised to meet their basic needs. In addition, the Indians caught diseases from the whites, and many Cheyenne children died. Pressed by these problems, Dull Knife and his people finally decided to sneak away and attempt to return to their homeland. On September 9, 1877, about three hundred Cheyenne quietly headed north. They crossed some 1,500 miles of plains on which many whites had settled. Meanwhile, more than ten thousand soldiers and three thousand white civilians chased the band northward. On several occasions the Indians became trapped but managed to escape.

The great Cheyenne chief, Dull Knife, led his people's courageous struggle for freedom.

Eventually the soldiers caught up with the Cheyenne. When army officials told them that they had to go back to Indian Country, some of the Indians, in despair, tried to run away. And during the bloody roundup that ensued, more than a hundred Cheyenne were killed. Later the government granted Dull Knife's band a small patch of land in Montana; but by that time, only about eighty members of the defiant little group were still alive.

superior advantages; but he has not created us to be your
slaves. *We are a separate people!*[59]

In the 1870s the famous Sioux chief Sitting Bull expressed ex-
plicit objections to both the reservation system and the Peace Policy,
saying, "I do not wish to be shut up in a corral. It is bad for young
men to be fed by an agent. It makes them lazy and drunken. All
[reservation] Indians I have seen are worthless. They are neither red
warriors nor white farmers."[60]

Resistance to Reservations and Assimilation

That Sitting Bull's sentiments were shared by many other Indians is
illustrated by the fact that even as Grant's new policy was being in-
stituted, various tribes and bands of Indians continued to resist both
white encroachment and forced assimilation. Sitting Bull himself
was involved in the most prominent and successful example of such
resistance—the defeat of Custer and the Seventh Cavalry at the Little Bighorn in 1876. As it happened, of course, the strategic importance of this Indian victory was nullified by subsequent events. For
reasons unknown, the tribes involved did not, as they should have,
remain united and follow up with coordinated attacks on other army
units in the region. Instead, they disbanded and went their separate
ways, virtually ensuring that the whites could continue their own rou-
tine strategy of picking them off one by one.

Also, and perhaps more importantly, Custer's defeat sent shock
waves through white society, which indignantly and angrily viewed
the battle as a "massacre" by "bloodthirsty savages." Such continued
armed resistance by the Indians only reinforced the opinion among a
majority of whites that forcing the Indians onto reservations was necessary. This led the U.S. government to step up its campaigns against
the Sioux and other western tribes. In the following decade or so, in
what proved to be the last phase of the American Indian Wars, one
tribe after another was surrounded, defeated, and subjugated, and
survivors were usually herded onto reservations. There they were expected to conform to Grant's new policy of assimilation, slowly but
surely to shed their very identities as Indians.

Yet even after such forced relocation, some tribes courageously
continued to resist. About a year after Custer's defeat, the Nez Percé,

During the 1870s and 1880s, isolated tribes of Indians attempted to evade whites; but U.S. soldiers hunted them, as illustrated in this drawing.

under Chief Joseph, escaped from their Idaho reservation and made a daring attempt to reach Canada, where they hoped to find freedom. After several times outwitting or fighting off the army units sent to capture them, they came within only thirty miles of achieving their goal; in the end, however, they had no choice but to surrender.

At the very same time that the Nez Percé made their bid for freedom, three hundred Cheyenne, led by Chief Dull Knife, escaped from their own reservation and tried to return to their ancestral lands in Montana. With some ten thousand soldiers and three thousand white civilians chasing them, the small band traveled over fifteen hundred miles before being cornered and captured.

Groups of Apache warriors in the deserts of New Mexico and Arizona also refused at first to be confined on reservations and begin assimilation. Under their war leader Geronimo, the Chiricahua Apache waged effective guerrilla warfare against the U.S. Army throughout the late 1870s and early 1880s. Geronimo managed to hold out until 1886, when an army of five thousand, led by General George Crook, forced him to surrender, an event that finally made it safe for massive white settlement of the Southwest.

This famous photo of the Apache war chief Geronimo was taken long after he ceased to be a threat to the whites.

The Ghost Dance and Wounded Knee

The final major battle of the Indian Wars, which took place four years later, was a last gasp attempt by the Indians to resist the ongoing white policy of reservations and assimilation and keep their own cultural traditions intact. Sensing that their civilization was nearing extinction, in desperation many Indians resorted to an unusual new religious belief that promised the salvation of their race. Called the Ghost Dance, it became popular on most of the Plains reservations in 1890. It predicted that, through magical powers, many whites would die and the Indians would push the rest eastward into the ocean. What is more, the leaders of the Ghost Dance claimed, wearing special shirts during the faith's ceremonies would make Indians immune to white soldiers' bullets. In a speech to his followers, one of these leaders, Short Bull, a Sioux, declared:

> If the soldiers surround you four deep, three of you, on whom I have put holy shirts, will sing a song, which I have taught you, around them, when some of them will drop dead. Then the rest will start to run, but their horses will sink into the earth. The riders will jump from their horses, but they will sink into the earth also. Then you can do as you desire with them. Now, you must know this, that all the soldiers and that race will be dead. There will be only five thousand of them left living on earth. My friends and relations, this is straight and true.[61]

U.S. Army leaders feared that the Ghost Dance would lead to new Indian uprisings. So soldiers began arresting Ghost Dance leaders.

Members of the Oglala Sioux perform the Ghost Dance. This effort to resist white encroachment and defeat of the tribes failed.

The climax of this campaign occurred in late December 1890, when U.S. cavalry units surrounded a group of Sioux, including a number of Ghost Dancers, along Wounded Knee Creek in South Dakota. During the attempt to arrest the Indians, someone—whether a soldier or an Indian is unknown—fired a weapon, initiating a killing spree in which the soldiers fired repeatedly at unarmed men, women, and children. A few minutes later, 153 Indians, including the group's leader, Chief Big Foot, lay dead.

A Terrible Toll

In the wake of Wounded Knee, with military resistance by Native Americans at an end, the U.S. government could now concentrate all of its Indian-related activities on its assimilation efforts. Overall, forced removal and relocation of various tribes had already taken an awful toll. Virtually all American Indians were now confined on reservations in various parts of the country. White officials proceeded to restrict the reservation Indians' freedom of movement, forbade them from governing themselves, and curtailed their religious freedom. U.S. officials could and often did arrest traditional tribal lead-

After the massacre at Wounded Knee, in December 1890, Chief Big Foot lies dead and frozen on the site of this last major armed conflict of the Indian Wars.

INDIAN LAND FOR SALE

GET A HOME
OF
YOUR OWN
❉
EASY PAYMENTS

PERFECT TITLE
❉
POSSESSION
WITHIN
THIRTY DAYS

FINE LANDS IN THE WEST

IRRIGATED		AGRICULTURAL
IRRIGABLE	GRAZING	DRY FARMING

IN 1910 THE DEPARTMENT OF THE INTERIOR SOLD UNDER SEALED BIDS ALLOTTED INDIAN LAND AS FOLLOWS:

Location.	Acres.	Average Price per Acre.	Location.	Acres.	Average Price per Acre.
Colorado	5,211.21	$7.27	Oklahoma	34,664.00	$19.14
Idaho	17,013.00	24.85	Oregon	1,020.00	15.43
Kansas	1,684.50	33.45	South Dakota	120,445.00	16.53
Montana	11,034.00	9.86	Washington	4,879.00	41.37
Nebraska	5,641.00	36.65	Wisconsin	1,069.00	17.00
North Dakota	22,610.70	9.93	Wyoming	865.00	20.64

FOR THE YEAR 1911 IT IS ESTIMATED THAT **350,000** ACRES WILL BE OFFERED FOR SALE

For information as to the character of the land write for booklet, "INDIAN LANDS FOR SALE," to the Superintendent U. S. Indian School at any one of the following places:

CALIFORNIA: Hoopa.	MINNESOTA: Onigum.	NORTH DAKOTA: Fort Totten.	OKLAHOMA—Con. Sac and Fox Agency.	SOUTH DAKOTA: Cheyenne Agency.	WASHINGTON: Fort Simcoe.
COLORADO: Ignacio.	MONTANA: Crow Agency.	Fort Yates. OKLAHOMA:	Shawnee. Wyandotte.	Crow Creek. Greenwood.	Fort Spokane. Tekoa.
IDAHO: Lapwai.	NEBRASKA: Macy.	Anadarko. Cantonment.	OREGON: Klamath Agency.	Lower Brule. Pine Ridge.	Tulalip. WISCONSIN:
KANSAS: Horton.	Santee.	Colony. Darlington.	Pendleton. Roseburg.	Rosebud. Sisseton.	Oneida.
Nadeau.	Winnebago.	Muskogee, Pawnee.	Siletz.		

WALTER L. FISHER,
Secretary of the Interior.

ROBERT G. VALENTINE,
Commissioner of Indian Affairs.

The 1887 General Allotment Act allowed the government to sell off parts of Native American reservations to white homesteaders.

ers and healers, often without just cause, while simultaneously allowing Christian missionaries to roam freely on the reservations, attempting to convert Indians to white beliefs and ways.

Meanwhile the allotment concept, intended to turn Indians into homesteaders in the white mold, was put into practice. In 1887, shortly before the Wounded Knee massacre, Congress passed the

General Allotment Act (or Dawes Act), which partitioned the reservations into individual parcels. But the bill also allowed the government to sell off "surplus tracts" to white settlers, which caused many reservations steadily to shrink. By the early 1930s, reservation land holdings had fallen from 138 million to 48 million acres.

At the same time, the reservation system failed to protect Native Americans' interests. They were not allowed to have their own local reservation governments, for instance. And for many decades, the vast majority of Indians living on the remaining reservation lands suffered from the cruel effects of white racism, inferior educational and health care facilities, and extreme, grinding poverty.

A change for the better, from the Native American point of view, came with the 1934 Indian Reorganization Act. It reversed the policy of assimilation and allotment and for the first time allowed Indians to form their own reservation governments. Carl Waldman explains:

> Under socially progressive President Franklin D. Roosevelt and his commissioner of Indian Affairs, John Collier . . . Congress passed the Indian Reorganization Act . . . [which] gave legal sanction to tribal holdings; resumed [gave back] unsold allotted lands to tribes; made provisions for the purchase of new lands; encouraged tribal constitutions, systems of justice, and business corporations; expanded educational opportunities through new facilities and loans . . . advocated the hiring of Indians by the Bureau of Indian Affairs and Indian involvement in management and policy-making at national and tribal levels . . . and granted Indians religious freedom.[62]

The new policy did help many Indians take some initial steps toward self-determination and renewed dignity as a people with their own identity. However, it was by no means a cure-all for the numerous problems by then faced by American Indians. Years of wrongheaded, exploitative policy, mismanagement, neglect, and out-and-out corruption and racism on the part of U.S. government agents and officials had taken a terrible toll; living conditions on most Indian reservations were substandard, while social and occupational opportunities for Indians, both on and off the reservations, were limited. Moreover, the federal government still oversaw the reservations and

The Rise of Indian Protesters

Improvements in living conditions and job opportunities for Indians came only very slowly in the early decades of the twentieth century. And for a long time, most Indians dared not speak out too loudly for their rights, for fear of reprisals by white society and authorities. Beginning in the late 1960s, however, a number of college-educated members of various Indian communities formed organizations and civil rights groups to protest conditions on the reservations. One of the most important was the American Indian Movement (AIM), founded in 1968 in Minneapolis by three Chippewa—Dennis Banks, George Mitchell, and Clyde Bellecourt—and a Sioux—Russell Means. In 1969 members of AIM occupied Alcatraz Island (site of a famous prison in San Francisco Bay), gaining worldwide attention and support for their efforts. Another dramatic protest, called the "Trail of Broken Treaties," occurred in 1972, when Indian rights activists occupied the offices of the Bureau of Indian Affairs in Washington, D.C. A year later a group of Indians and whites seized the village of Wounded Knee, South Dakota, to call attention to Indian problems. Indian activists continue on a periodic basis to pressure the U.S. government for social recognition and economic reparations.

In the late 1960s, supporters of the American Indian Movement (AIM) protest the substandard conditions on Indian reservations.

wielded authority over many aspects of Indian life. And agents of the
Bureau of Indian Affairs continued to manage many Indian activities.
In addition, in the late 1940s and on into the 1950s, the government
reintroduced various assimilation programs, including one designed
to get Indians to leave their reservations and move to big cities.

The Key to Renewal

Federal efforts to assimilate Native Americans finally halted in the
1960s. And from that time to the present, U.S. Indian policy has,
at least in principle, been committed to the idea of true Indian self-
determination. Beginning in earnest in the 1970s, Indian activists
(demonstrators, court litigants, lawyers, politicians, and so on), as
well as whites who sympathized with their causes, pushed (and
continue to push) for an improvement in the treatment of and opportunities for Indians. Among the concepts and goals of both
many government officials and activists, says Waldman, are

> tribal restoration, self-government, cultural renewal, devel-
> opment of reservation resources, and self-efficiency, as well
> as the . . . provision of economic and social programs needed
> to raise the standard of living of Indian peoples to a level
> comparable to the rest of society. The thrust of the policy of
> course has varied with changing federal administrations.
> And Indian leaders themselves have advocated varying as-
> pects of it . . . which expresses Indian involvement and
> choice.[63]

As the twenty-first century dawns, both Indians and whites work
to make these goals a reality and achieve true equality and justice for
Native Americans. Unfortunately, the horrors and devastation wrought
in past centuries cannot easily or completely be erased. But the principal focus of modern Native Americans is on the present and the future.
Most want to do the best they can for themselves and their families in
a world still largely controlled by whites, while maintaining their identity and dignity as a separate people. N. Scott Momaday, whose father
was a Kiowa and mother a Cherokee, and who won the Pulitzer Prize
in 1968 for his novel *House Made of Dawn*—puts it this way:

> It's very hard to be specific about how to change the future.
> The major issues we face now are survival—how to live in

the modern world. Part of that is how to remain Indian, how to assimilate without ceasing to be an Indian. I think some important strides have been made. Indians remain Indian, and against pretty good odds [including white attempts to assimilate and eradicate them]. They remain Indians and, in some situations, by a thread. Their languages are being lost at a tremendous rate, [and] poverty is rampant. . . . But still there are Indians and the traditional [Indian] world is still intact.[64]

Despite the enormous pain and sorrow of their defeat and its difficult aftermath, therefore, most surviving Native Americans persevere in maintaining their self-identity. This will continue to be an important key to their renewal over the course of future generations.

Notes

Introduction: "Our Indian Life Is Gone Forever"

1. Quoted in Thomas Jefferson, *Notes on the State of Virginia*, published as William Peden, ed., *Notes on the State of Virginia by Thomas Jefferson*. New York: Norton, 1972, p. 63.
2. Russell Thornton, *American Indian Holocaust and Survival: A Population History Since 1492*. Norman: University of Oklahoma Press, 1987, p. 49.
3. John Tebbel and Keith Jennison, *The American Indian Wars*. New York: Harper and Brothers, 1960, p. 1.
4. Quoted in Peter Nabokov, ed., *Native American Testimony*. New York: Harper and Row, 1978, p. 182.

Chapter 1: The Eve of War: Cultural Differences Between Indians and Whites

5. Nabokov, *Native American Testimony*, p. 69.
6. From a letter written in the early 1780s to *Freeman's Journal*, quoted in Wilcomb E. Washburn, ed., *The Indian and the White Man*. Garden City, NY: Doubleday, 1964, p. 116.
7. Quoted in Washburn, *The Indian and the White Man*, p. 210.
8. Quoted in Washburn, *The Indian and the White Man*, pp. 212–13.
9. George E. Tinker, "Religion," in Frederick E. Hoxie, ed., *Encyclopedia of North American Indians*. Boston: Houghton Mifflin, 1996, pp. 537–39.
10. Quoted in Annette Rosensteil, *Red and White: Indian Views of the White Man, 1492–1982*. New York: Universe Books, 1983, pp.116–17.
11. Quoted in Francis P. Prucha, *American Indian Policy in the Formative Years: The Indian Trade and Intercourse Acts, 1790–1834*.

Cambridge, MA: Harvard University Press, 1962, p. 162.
12. Nabokov, *Native American Testimony*, p. 70.
13. Anthony F. C. Wallace, *Jefferson and the Indians: The Tragic Fate of the First Americans*. Cambridge, MA: Harvard University Press, 1999, p. 205.

Chapter 2: Manifest Destiny: White Expansion into Indian Lands

14. Quoted in Charles L. Sanford, ed., *Manifest Destiny and the Imperialism Question*. New York: John Wiley and Sons, 1974, p. 28.
15. Quoted in Robert W. Johannsen, *The Halls of Montezumas*. New York: Oxford University Press, 1985, pp. 292–93.
16. Quoted in Washburn, *Indian and the White Man*, pp. 125–26.
17. Theodore Roosevelt, *The Winning of the West (1889–1896)*, quoted in Edward H. Spicer, *A Short History of the Indians of the United States*. New York: D. Van Nostrand, 1969, pp. 237–39.
18. Quoted in T. C. McLuhan, ed., *Touch the Earth: A Self-Portrait of Indian Existence*. New York: Promontory Press, 1971, p. 54.
19. Quoted in A. A. Lipscomb and A. E. Bergh, eds., *The Writings of Thomas Jefferson*. 20 vols. Washington, DC: Thomas Jefferson Memorial Association of U.S., 1903, vol. 10, p. 369.
20. Quoted in Rosenstiel, *Red and White*, p. 114.
21. Quoted in Nabokov, *Native American Testimony*, p. 118.
22. Quoted in Nabokov, *Native American Testimony*, p. 120.
23. Nabokov, *Native American Testimony*, p. 120.
24. Quoted in Wallace, *Jefferson and the Indians*, p. 165.

Chapter 3: Tears for Tecumseh: The Lost Cause of Indian Unity

25. Dale Van Every, *The Disinherited: The Lost Birthright of the American Indian*. New York: Morrow, 1976, pp. 23–24.
26. Quoted in *American State Papers, Indian Affairs, Vol. 1*. Washington, DC: Gales and Seaton, 1832, p. 650.
27. Stephen E. Ambrose, *Undaunted Courage: Meriwether Lewis, Thomas Jefferson, and the Opening of the American West*. New York: Simon and Schuster, 1996, p. 337.
28. Quoted in Frederick W. Turner, ed., *The Portable North American Indian Reader*. New York: Viking, 1974, p. 247.
29. Carl Waldman, *Atlas of the North American Indian*. New York:

Facts On File, 1985, p.115.

30. Quoted in Nabokov, *Native American Testimony*, pp. 96–98.

31. Quoted in Turner, *Portable North American Indian Reader*, p. 246.

Chapter 4: Removal and Relocation: A Systematic Policy of Subjugation

32. Van Every, *The Disinherited*, p.18.

33. Howard Zinn, *A People's History of the United States*. New York: HarperCollins, 1980, p. 124.

34. Quoted in Wallace, *Jefferson and the Indians*, p. 273.

35. Zinn, *People's History*, p.125.

36. Peter Farb, *Man's Rise to Civilization as Shown by the Indians of North America from Primeval Times to the Coming of the Industrial State*. New York: E. P. Dutton, 1968, pp. 300–1.

37. Quoted in Turner, *Portable North American Indian Reader*, pp. 249–50.

38. Van Every, *The Disinherited*, pp. 138–40.

39. Quoted in John Ehle, *Trail of Tears: The Rise and Fall of the Cherokee Nation*. New York: Doubleday, 1988, pp. 275–78.

40. Quoted in Ehle, *Trail of Tears*, pp. 357–58.

41. Quoted in Van Every, *The Disinherited*, p. 270.

Chapter 5: White Logistical Advantages: The Conquest of the Western Indians

42. Nabokov, *Native American Testimony*, p. 95.

43. Benjamin Capps, *The Indians*. New York: Time-Life Books, 1973, p. 58.

44. Capps, *Indians*, p. 58.

45. Quoted in Nabokov, *Native American Testimony*, p. 93.

46. Alan Axelrod, *Chronicle of the Indian Wars, from Colonial Times to Wounded Knee*. New York: Prentice-Hall, 1993, p. 181.

47. Axelrod, *Chronicle of the Indian Wars*, p. 181.

48. Arrell M. Gibson, *The American Indian: Prehistory to the Present*. Lexington, MA: D. C. Heath, 1980, pp. 50–51.

49. Tom Holm, "Wars: 1850–1900," in Hoxie, *Encyclopedia of North American Indians*, p. 673.

50. See William O. Taylor, *With Custer on the Little Bighorn*. New York: Viking, 1996.

51. Quoted in Edgar I. Stewart, *Custer's Luck*. Norman: University

of Oklahoma Press, 1955, p. 459.

52. Quoted in Dee Brown, *Bury My Heart at Wounded Knee: An Indian History of the American West*. New York: Holt, Rinehart and Winston, 1970, p. 296.

Chapter 6: Assimilation Versus Self-Identity: The Final Defeat and Its Aftermath

53. Ward Churchill, *A Little Matter of Genocide: Holocaust Denial in the Americas, 1492 to the Present*. San Francisco: City Light Books, 1997, p. 245.

54. Quoted in Churchill, *A Little Matter of Genocide*, p. 245.

55. Quoted in Wallace, *Jefferson and the Indians*, p. 317.

56. Quoted in Wallace, *Jefferson and the Indians*, p. 223.

57. Quoted in Henry E. Fritz, *The Movement for Indian Assimilation, 1860–1890*. Philadelphia: University of Pennsylvania Press, 1963, p. 81.

58. Axelrod, *Chronicle of the Indian Wars*, p. 212.

59. Quoted in Nabokov, *Native American Testimony*, p. 123.

60. Quoted in Nabokov, *Native American Testimony*, p. 192.

61. Quoted in Spicer, *Short History of the Indians*, pp. 282–83.

62. Waldman, *Atlas of the North American Indian*, pp. 192–94.

63. Waldman, *Atlas of the North American Indian*, p.195.

64. Quoted in Nabokov, *Native American Testimony*, p. 438.

Chronology

1607
About nine hundred English settlers establish the colony of Jamestown, on the shore of Chesapeake Bay in what is now Virginia. They are greeted and aided by the local Indians.

1743
Thomas Jefferson, who will later advocate moving eastern Indian tribes across the Mississippi, is born in Virginia.

1754–63
The years of the French and Indian War, fought between Britain and France and their respective colonists and Indian allies.

1759–60
The Cherokee fight with white settlers on the Carolina frontier.

1768
Tecumseh, the noted Shawnee advocate of Indian unity, is born near the present site of Springfield, Ohio.

1775–83
The years of the American Revolution. In 1776 the British colonists declare their independence from the mother country, giving birth to the United States.

1790
The Shawnee, Miami, and other tribes join forces under Chief Little Turtle to defeat an army of fourteen hundred U.S. troops in the Ohio Valley. The same Indians defeat another U.S. force the following year.

1794
General Anthony Wayne defeats a large force of Indians, Tecumseh

among them, in the Battle of Fallen Timbers, after which thousands of white settlers begin pouring into Ohio and Indiana.

1803
Led by President Thomas Jefferson, the United States purchases the territory of Louisiana from France, roughly doubling the size of the country. This acquisition, followed up by the Lewis and Clark expedition (1803–6), which explores the continent's western lands, initiates a new movement of white westward expansion into Indian-inhabited regions.

1808
Tecumseh and his brother, "the Prophet," establish Prophet's Town, a village incorporating Indians from several tribes, on the Wabash River in Indiana.

1812
War commences between the United States and Britain. Hoping to halt further U.S. expansion, Tecumseh and other Indian leaders ally themselves with the British.

1813
Tecumseh is killed in battle, effectively ending chances for a large pan-Indian crusade against the United States.

1813–14
The years of the Creek Wars, in which the United States defeats the Creek and forces most of them to move to Indian Country (encompassing much of what are now Missouri and Oklahoma), a region set aside for Indian relocation.

1821
Those Cherokee forced to relocate to Indian Country go to war with the Osage, who already occupy the region.

ca. 1829
Goyathlay, the Apache war leader who will come to be known by the name given him by the Mexicans—Geronimo—is born.

1835
President Andrew Jackson publicly warns those Cherokee who have refused to relocate that they must do so or face dire consequences.

1835–42
Some three thousand Seminole are shipped from Florida to Indian Country.

1838
U.S. troops forcibly remove the remaining Cherokee from their homes and lead them in a cruel forced march overland to Indian Country, an incident that becomes known as the "Trail of Tears."

1848
The Apache, Navajo, and many other Indians inhabiting the arid Southwest (what are now Arizona, New Mexico, and Southern California) come under U.S. jurisdiction with the signing of the treaty ending the Mexican-American War.

1860–65
The years of the American Civil War.

1864
The United States defeats the Navajo and forces them to march to a relocation camp in eastern New Mexico. A Colorado regiment led by Colonel John M. Chivington massacres a group of Cheyenne and Arapaho at Sand Creek, in southeastern Colorado.

1876
The Sioux, aided by the Cheyenne and other Plains Indians, defeat General George Crook's forces at Rosebud Creek, in southeastern Montana. A few days later, at the nearby Little Bighorn River, the allied Indians wipe out a force of over two hundred troops led by George Armstrong Custer.

1877
Several hundred Nez Percé Indians, led by Chief Joseph, flee their assigned reservation in an attempt to reach Canada and freedom. They are captured when only thirty miles from their goal. Meanwhile, some three hundred Cheyenne, led by Chief Dull Knife, attempt to return to their ancestral lands in Montana. They too are captured before attaining their goal.

1886
After many years of waging highly effective guerrilla warfare against frustrated U.S. troops, the last undefeated bands of Apache surrender.

1887

The U.S. Congress passes the General Allotment Act (or Dawes Act), which provides for dividing up Indian reservations into tiny parcels to be homesteaded by Indian families.

1890

The Ghost Dance, a new religion that promises the destruction of the whites and salvation of the Indian race, spreads across the western plains. Sitting Bull, legendary Sioux chief, is shot and killed while being arrested on suspicion of inciting Indians to join the Ghost Dance. Soon afterward U.S. troops massacre a large group of unarmed Indians at Wounded Knee Creek in South Dakota.

1934

Congress passes the Indian Reorganization Act, which ends allotment, reverses many of the Indian assimilation policies of the previous several decades, and allows Indians to form their own tribal governments on their reservations.

1973

Members of the American Indian Movement (AIM), a militant activist organization demanding better treatment for Indians, occupy the Pine Ridge Reservation, site of the Wounded Knee massacre, for seventy-one days. Two years later two FBI agents are killed in a shoot-out with Indian activists on the same reservation.

1978

Congress passes the American Indian Religious Freedom Act, guaranteeing protection for Indian religious beliefs under the First Amendment.

For Further Reading

Kae Cheatham, *Dennis Banks: Native American Activist.* Berkeley Heights, NJ: Enslow, 1997. A general biography of one of the most important Native American figures of the twentieth century (who was a cofounder of the American Indian Movement, or AIM, in 1968).

Stan Hoig, *The Cheyenne.* New York: Chelsea House, 1990. This is a worthwhile introduction to one of the most famous of the western Plains tribes, which was defeated by the U.S. Army in the nineteenth century. The most famous episode was that of a Cheyenne band led by Chief Dull Knife, which made a daring bid for freedom after being consigned to a reservation.

Stuart A. Kallen and Deanne Durrett, *Native American Chiefs and Warriors.* San Diego: Lucent Books, 1999. Part of Lucent's History Makers series, this book is loaded with valuable information about some of the more important Native American leaders during the American Indian Wars.

Allison Lassieur, *Before the Storm: American Indians Before the Europeans.* New York: Facts on File, 1998. An informative, fascinating examination of Indian life and customs on the eve of European colonization. The author includes some excellent material gathered by modern archaeologists.

Catherine J. Long, *The Cherokee.* San Diego: Lucent Books, 2000. A fine overview of the background, struggles, and customs of the tribe that endured the deprivations of Indian removal, including the infamous Trail of Tears.

Judith Simpson, *Native Americans.* New York: Time-Life Books, 1995. This is a beautifully illustrated general look at Native American cultures.

Michael Bad Hand Terry, *Daily Life in a Plains Indian Village 1868.* Boston: Houghton Mifflin, 1999. A very colorful and informative synopsis of the way the Plains Indians lived at the time of their conquest by the United States.

Author's Note: For those more ambitious young readers, I recommend beginning with Carl Waldman's *Atlas of the North American Indian* (New York: Facts On File, 1985), an excellent summary of North American Indian civilization; Alan Axelrod's *Chronicle of the Indian Wars* (New York: Prentice-Hall, 1993) is a good general synopsis of the Indian Wars; for more specific, detailed information, I recommend Dee Brown's *Bury My Heart at Wounded Knee* (New York: Holt, Rinehart and Winston, 1970), Dale Van Every's *The Disinherited* (New York: Morrow, 1976), and Henry E. Fritz's *The Movement for Indian Assimilation* (Philadelphia: University of Pennsylvania Press, 1963), all on an advanced reading level but extremely worthwhile and eye-opening. Among the studies of individual Indian figures, John Sugden's *Tecumseh: A Life* (New York: Henry Holt, 1997) is a masterful and moving account of the life of a truly remarkable person.

Works Consulted

Dee Brown, *Bury My Heart at Wounded Knee: An Indian History of the American West.* New York: Holt, Rinehart and Winston, 1970. This overview of the destruction of Indian civilization by the United States remains one of the best and most powerful books on the subject. Highly recommended.

Ward Churchill, *A Little Matter of Genocide: Holocaust Denial in the Americas, 1492 to the Present.* San Francisco: City Light Books, 1997. A somewhat scholarly volume that makes a strong case for calling what the United States did to the Indians genocide.

Brian W. Dippie, *The Vanishing American: White Attitudes and U.S. Indian Policy.* Middletown, CT: Wesleyan University Press, 1982. A well-informed examination of how the U.S. government and white Americans in general viewed the Indians and from such views shaped official policy affecting Native Americans.

Grant Foreman, *Indian Removal.* Norman: University of Oklahoma Press, 1972. A worthwhile overview of the unfortunate and destructive policy of uprooting the Indians from their ancestral homelands.

Henry E. Fritz, *The Movement for Indian Assimilation, 1860–1890.* Philadelphia: University of Pennsylvania Press, 1963. This is a very well-researched, informative, and absorbing examination of the paternalistic, patronizing, and ultimately destructive American policy of attempting to assimilate Indians into white culture.

Frederick E. Hoxie, ed., *Encyclopedia of North American Indians.* Boston: Houghton Mifflin, 1996. A large, highly informative overview of the tribes, leaders, experiences, and

113

problems of Native Americans, including much about the twentieth century.

Albert L. Hurtado and Peter Iverson, eds., *Major Problems in American Indian History*. Lexington, MA: D. C. Heath, 1994. This well-written book examines many of the reasons for the defeat of the Indians by the whites.

Peter C. Mancall and James H. Merrill, eds., *American Encounters: Natives and Newcomers from European Contact to Indian Removal, 1500–1850*. New York: Routledge, 2000. An excellent collection of essays by noted historians and other experts about the destruction of Native American civilization.

Paula M. Marks, *In a Barren Land: American Indian Dispossession and Survival*. New York: Morrow, 1998. An effective look at how various tribes had to cope with losing their old way of life and starting new lives in the areas the U.S. government allotted for them.

S. L. A. Marshall, *Crimsoned Prairie: The Wars Between the United States and the Plains Indians During the Winning of the West*. New York: Scribner's, 1972. One of the more informative and moving overviews of the wars between the United States and the Plains Indians.

Peter Nabokov, ed., *Native American Testimony*. New York: Harper and Row, 1978. One of the best existing collections of original documents pertaining to the history and struggle of the Native Americans.

Edward H. Spicer, *A Short History of the Indians of the United States*. New York: D. Van Nostrand, 1969. This readable little history contains an extensive collection of primary source documents about Native Americans.

John Sugden, *Tecumseh: A Life*. New York: Henry Holt, 1997. Sugden delivers a powerful, extremely well-researched study of the famous chief who tried to create a Native American alliance against white expansion. Contains many insights into why the Indians lost their struggle with the whites. Highly recommended.

John Tebbel and Keith Jennison, *The American Indian Wars*. New York: Harper and Brothers, 1960. This is a very well-researched, well-documented, and well-written synopsis of the Indian Wars.

Russell Thornton, *American Indian Holocaust and Survival: A Population History Since 1492*. Norman: University of Oklahoma Press, 1987. A somewhat scholarly, nevertheless graphic and powerful study of the actual loss of life and property suffered by Native Americans in their long struggle for survival against encroaching white civilization. Highly recommended for serious students of the subject.

George E. Tinker, *Missionary Conquest: The Gospel and Native American Cultural Genocide*. Minneapolis, MN: Fortress Press, 1993. This informative book by a Native American who is also a Christian minister examines the destructive effects of the misguided white policy of attempting to Christianize the Indians. Highly recommended for serious students of the struggles of Native Americans.

Frederick W. Turner, ed., *The Portable North American Indian Reader*. New York: Viking, 1974. An excellent collection of original documents about and quotes by Native Americans.

Dale Van Every, *The Disinherited: The Lost Birthright of the American Indian*. New York: Morrow, 1976. This powerful look at Indian removal and relocation, which includes numerous excerpts from primary sources, is one of the best books ever written about the Indians.

Carl Waldman, *Atlas of the North American Indian*. New York: Facts On File, 1985. This is a general but very useful reference work summarizing the various North American Indian tribes and their civilization.

Anthony F. C. Wallace, *Jefferson and the Indians: The Tragic Fate of the First Americans*. Cambridge, MA: Harvard University Press, 1999. Award-winning anthropologist and historian Anthony Wallace has produced a superlative examination of the motives and policies of President Jefferson and his colleagues regarding the "problem" of what to do about Native Americans in the early years of the United States. The major reasons for the defeat of the Indians by the whites become clear as Wallace explores, with impressive documentation, the early stages of the formulation of U.S. Indian policy. Very highly recommended.

———, *The Long, Bitter Trail: Andrew Jackson and the Indians*. New York: Hill and Wang, 1993. A thoughtful telling by a fine

scholar of how Jackson pushed for and achieved wholesale removal of various Native American tribes from their homelands.

Wilcomb E. Washburn, ed., *The Indian and the White Man*. Garden
City, NY: Doubleday, 1964. Contains many fascinating primary sources relating to various Native American tribes and
their leaders and experiences.

Additional Works Consulted

Stephen E. Ambrose, *Undaunted Courage: Meriwether Lewis, Thomas Jefferson, and the Opening of the American West.* New York: Simon and Schuster, 1996.

American State Papers, Indian Affairs, Vol. 1. Washington, DC: Gales and Seaton, 1832.

Alan Axelrod, *Chronicle of the Indian Wars, from Colonial Times to Wounded Knee.* New York: Prentice-Hall, 1993.

Betty Ballantine and Ian Ballantine, eds., *The Native Americans: An Illustrated History.* Atlanta: Turner, 1992.

Norman Bancroft-Hunt, *Warriors: Warfare and the Native American Indian.* London: Salamander Books, 1995.

Nancy B. Black and Bette S. Weidman, eds., *White of Red: Images of the American Indian.* Port Washington, NY: Kennikat Press, 1976.

Julian P. Boyd et al., eds., *The Papers of Thomas Jefferson.* Princeton, NJ: Princeton University Press, 1950.

Cyrus T. Brady, *Indian Fights and Fighters.* Lincoln: University of Nebraska Press, 1971.

Ray Brandes, ed., *Troopers West: Military and Indian Affairs on the American Frontier.* San Diego: Frontier Heritage Press, 1970.

Benjamin Capps, *The Indians.* New York: Time-Life Books, 1973.

Paul H. Carlson, *The Plains Indians.* College Station: Texas A & M University Press, 1998.

David H. Cockran, *The Cherokee Frontier, Conflict and Survival.* Norman: University of Oklahoma Press, 1962.

Evan S. Connell, *Son of the Morning Star: Custer and the Little Bighorn.* San Francisco: North Point Press, 1984.

R. S. Cotterill, *The Southern Indians: The Story of the Civilized Tribes Before Removal.* Norman: University of Oklahoma Press, 1954.

Carlton Culmsee, *Utah's Black Hawk War.* Logan: Utah State University Press, 1973.

Angie Debo, *A History of the Indians of the U.S.* Norman: University of Oklahoma Press, 1970.

Vine Deloria Jr., *Behind the Trail of Broken Treaties: An Indian Declaration of Independence.* New York: Delacorte Press, 1974.

———, *Custer Died for Your Sins: An Indian Manifesto.* New York: Macmillan, 1969.

———, *God Is Red: A Native View of Religion.* Golden, CO: Fulcrum, 1994.

Gregory E. Dowd, *A Spirited Resistance: The North American Indian Struggle for Unity, 1745–1815.* Baltimore: Johns Hopkins University Press, 1992.

John Ehle, *Trail of Tears: The Rise and Fall of the Cherokee Nation.* New York: Doubleday, 1988.

Joseph Ellis, *American Sphinx: The Character of Thomas Jefferson.* New York: Knopf, 1997.

Peter Farb, *Man's Rise to Civilization as Shown by the Indians of North America from Primeval Times to the Coming of the Industrial State.* New York: E. P. Dutton, 1968.

T. R. Fehrenbach, *Comanches: The Destruction of a People.* New York: Da Capo, 1994.

Grant Foreman, *Indian Removal.* Norman: University of Oklahoma Press, 1953.

Arrell M. Gibson, *The American Indian: Prehistory to the Present.* Lexington, MA: D. C. Heath, 1980.

Daniel Gookin, *Historical Collections of the Indians in New England.* N.P.: Towtaid, 1970.

Jerome A. Greene, ed., *Battles and Skirmishes of the Great Sioux War, 1876–1877: A Military View.* Norman: University of Oklahoma Press, 1993.

Robert S. Grumet, ed., *Northeastern Indian Lives, 1632–1816.* Amherst: University of Massachusetts Press, 1996.

Royal B. Hassrick, *The Colorful Story of North American Indians.* London: Octopus Books, 1974.

Lawrence M. Hauptman, *The Iroquois Struggle for Survival.* Syracuse, NY: Syracuse University Press, 1986.

Jamake Highwater, *Fodor's Indian America.* New York: David McKay, 1975.

Stanley Hoig, *The Sand Creek Massacre.* Norman: University of Oklahoma Press, 1961.

Jason Hook, *American Indian Warrior Chiefs: Tecumseh, Crazy Horse, Chief Joseph, Geronimo.* Dorset, UK: Firebird Books, 1990.

Helen A. Howard, *Saga of Chief Joseph.* Lincoln: University of Nebraska Press, 1965.

George Hyde, *Indians of the High Plains.* Norman: University of Oklahoma Press, 1959.

Wilbur R. Jacobs, *Dispossessing the American Indian: Indians and Whites on the Colonial Frontier.* New York: Scribner's, 1972.

Robert W. Johannsen, *The Halls of Montezumas.* New York: Oxford University Press, 1985.

Alvin M. Josephy Jr., *The Indian Heritage of America.* New York: Knopf, 1968.

John Keegan, *Fields of Battle: The Wars for North America.* New York: Knopf, 1996.

A. A. Lipscomb and A. E. Bergh, eds., *The Writings of Thomas Jefferson.* 20 vols. Washington, DC: Thomas Jefferson Memorial Association of U.S., 1903.

Stephen Longstreet, *War Cries on Horseback: The Story of the Indian Wars of the Great Plains.* New York: W. H. Allen, 1971.

Dumas Malone, *Jefferson and His Time.* 6 vols. Boston: Little, Brown, 1948–1977.

T. C. McLuhan, ed., *Touch the Earth: A Self-Portrait of Indian Existence.* New York: Promontory Press, 1971.

Beatrice Medicine and Patricia Albers, *The Hidden Half: Studies of Plains Indian Women.* Lanham, MD: University Press of America, 1983.

Lee Miller, ed., *From the Heart: Voices of the American Indian.* New York: Random House, 1995.

James Mooney, *The Ghost Dance Religion and the Sioux Outbreak of 1890.* Lincoln: University of Nebraska Press, 1991.

Wayne Moquin, ed., *Great Documents in American Indian History*. New York: Da Capo, 1995.

J. Jay Myers, *Red Chiefs and White Challengers: Confrontations in American Indian History*. New York: Washington Square Press, 1971.

Roger L. Nichols and George R. Adams eds., *The American Indian: Past and Present*. Lexington, MA: Xerox College Publishing, 1971.

Wendell H. Ostwalt and Sharlotte Neely, *This Land Was Theirs: A Study of North American Indians*. Mountain View, CA: Mayfield, 1996.

Roger C. Owens et al., eds., *The North American Indians: A Sourcebook*. New York: Macmillan, 1967.

William Peden, ed., *Notes on the State of Virginia by Thomas Jefferson*. New York: Norton, 1972.

Howard Pekham, *Pontiac and the Indian Uprising of 1763*. Princeton, NJ: Princeton University Press, 1947.

Merrill Peterson, *Thomas Jefferson and the New Nation*. New York: Oxford University Press, 1970.

Francis P. Prucha, *American Indian Policy in the Formative Years: The Indian Trade and Intercourse Acts, 1790–1834*. Cambridge, MA: Harvard University Press, 1962.

Michael P. Rogin, *Fathers and Children: Andrew Jackson and the Subjugation of the American Indian*. New York: Knopf, 1975.

Annette Rosenstiel, *Red and White: Indian Views of the White Man, 1492–1982*. New York: Universe Books, 1983.

Helen C. Rountree, *Pocahontas's People: The Powhatan Indians of Virginia Through Four Centuries*. Norman: University of Oklahoma Press, 1990.

Charles C. Royce, *Indian Land Cessions in the United States, 18th Annual Report of the Bureau of American Ethnology*. Washington, DC: Government Printing Office, 1899.

Mari Sandoz, *Crazy Horse, the Strange Man of the Oglalas*. New York: Knopf, 1945.

Charles L. Sanford, ed., *Manifest Destiny and the Imperialism Question*. New York: John Wiley and Sons, 1974.

Raymond W. Steadman, *Shadows of the Indian: Stereotypes in American Culture*. Norman: University of Oklahoma Press, 1982.

Ian K. Steele, *Warpaths: Invasions of North America*. New York: Oxford University Press, 1994.

Edgar I. Stewart, *Custer's Luck*. Norman: University of Oklahoma Press, 1955.

Theodore Taylor, *The Bureau of Indian Affairs*. Boulder, CO: Westview Press, 1984.

William O. Taylor, *With Custer on the Little Bighorn*. New York: Viking, 1996.

Glen Tucker, *Tecumseh: Vision of Glory*. Indianapolis: Bobbs-Merrill, 1956.

William E. Unrau, *White Man's Wicked Water: The Alcohol Trade and Prohibition in Indian Country, 1802–1892*. Lawrence: University Press of Kansas, 1996.

Robert M. Utley, *The Last Days of the Sioux Nation*. New Haven: Yale University Press, 1963.

Robert M. Utley and Wilcomb E. Washburn, *Indian Wars*. Boston: Houghton Mifflin, 1977.

Wilcomb E. Washburn, *The Indian in America*. New York: Harper and Row, 1975.

Shirley H. Witt and Stan Steiner, eds., *The Way: An Anthology of American Indian Literature*. New York: Knopf, 1972.

Evelyn Wolfson, *From Abenaki to Zuni: A Dictionary of Native American Tribes*. New York: Walker, 1988.

Ronald Wright, *Stolen Continents: The Americas Through Indian Eyes Since 1492*. Boston: Houghton Mifflin, 1992.

Howard Zinn, *A People's History of the United States*. New York: HarperCollins, 1980.

Index

Picture Credits

About the Author

Historian and award-winning author Don Nardo has written many books for young adults about American history, including *The U.S. Presidency*, *The Mexican-American War*, *The Declaration of Independence*, and *Franklin D. Roosevelt: U.S. President*. Mr. Nardo lives with his wife, Christine, in Massachusetts.